Student Participation in Online Discussions

Khe Foon Hew · Wing Sum Cheung

Student Participation in Online Discussions

Challenges, Solutions, and Future Research

Springer

Khe Foon Hew
National Institute of Education, Learning Sciences, and Technologies
Nanyang Technological University
1 Nanyang Walk
Singapore 637616
Singapore

Wing Sum Cheung
National Institute of Education, Learning Sciences, and Technologies
Nanyang Technological University
1 Nanyang Walk
Singapore 637616
Singapore

ISBN 978-1-4614-2369-0 ISBN 978-1-4614-2370-6 (eBook)
DOI 10.1007/978-1-4614-2370-6
Springer New York Heidelberg Dordrecht London

Library of Congress Control Number: 2012939043

Printed on acid-free paper

Springer is part of Springer Science+Business Media (www.springer.com)

This book is dedicated to our Heavenly Father, family members, relatives, and friends

Foreword

From the elementary school to the college campus, the landscape of education is changing rapidly and dramatically due to technological advancements in bringing students and teachers in contact with one another beyond normal classroom hours. In higher education, a critical factor has been efforts by colleges and universities to increase enrollments and reduce costs of instruction by expanding distance learning opportunities via online and hybrid courses. In K-12 education, federal policies associated with the No Child Left Behind (NCLB) act of 2001, impose stringent accountability demands on schools, principals, and teachers for demonstrating student proficiency on state assessments. Classroom time is at a premium for covering the tested curricula. The consequence of these trends is rapidly decreasing opportunities for students to participate in face-to-face social learning activities important to their cognitive and personal development, such as discussion, group problem-solving, cooperative learning, and peer tutoring. An obvious solution is using technology to make such experiences available outside the regular classroom. But the newness of this application area, and the concomitant lack of research knowledge and practical experience by both teachers and instructional designers, have created uncertainties about best practices—until now.

Khe Foon Hew and Wing Sum Cheung, in the present book, Student Participation in Online Discussions: Challenges, Strategies, and Future Research, address the void in identifying and communicating research-based practices to increase the use and quality of online discussion. Importantly, they begin the book by developing, in the first two chapters, respectively, a strong theoretical rationale for student discussion and social learning activity as effective pedagogical strategies and an associated research framework supporting different approaches that have been validated in the literature. The argument created is both logical and compelling: (a) social learning activities make important contributions to students' development, (b) opportunities for social development will take place increasingly in asynchronous online contexts relative to in-person class discussions, but (c) student participation in online discussion tends to be limited due to student inhibitions, instructional design uncertainties, and contextual factors (e.g., uses of technology). In the remaining chapters, Hew and Cheung systematically address what appears to be the universe of possible problems limiting online discussions and offer remedies (via effective online supports and instructional strategies) for ensuring higher frequency and quality participation. The areas examined, to highlight only a few, include motivating students to participate and providing them appropriate support (e.g., on technical matters, time, content, etc.), course strategies such as grading and instructor facilitation, student versus instructor preferences, and audio discussion. Interspersed throughout the discussion of strategies are valuable case study examples that illustrate real-world applications. The book closes where it begins by encouraging use of research evidence as the basis for evaluating current practices and identifying new, more effective approaches.

Online discussions and social interactions will become increasingly pervasive in K-12 and higher education. In the pages to follow, Hew and Cheung provide valuable guidance in a thorough and highly readable manner to inform instructional design, course applications, and research.

Steven M. Ross
Johns Hopkins University

Preface

As a result of the widespread use of the Internet in schools and homes, asynchronous online discussion has become an increasingly common means of facilitating dialogue between instructors and students, and also between students and their peers beyond the boundaries of physical classrooms. Unfortunately, there are usually very few students who actively contribute in online discussions, and often student contribution in online discussions is limited. Why is limited student contribution observed in asynchronous online discussion? How can we alleviate this problem? The primary purpose of this book is to identify the various reasons or factors leading to limited student contribution in asynchronous online discussion, and to discuss the possible solutions or strategies that may address these limitations. These strategies are based upon empirical evidence.

This book is organized into three main sections. In the first section, we describe the characteristics of an asynchronous online discussion environment, as well as review over 110 empirical studies in order to identify the factors leading to limited student contribution. Limited student contribution is defined as students making few or no postings, students exhibiting surface-level thinking, or students displaying low-level knowledge construction in online discussions. We identified ten main factors: (a) not seeing the need for online discussion, (b) behavior or practice of instructor or participants, (c) personality traits, (d) difficulty in keeping up with the discussion, (e) not knowing what to contribute, (f) lack of critical thinking skills, (g) being content in merely answering queries, (h) technical aspects, (i) lack of time, and (j) not wanting to run the risk of being misunderstood.

In the second section, we describe empirically based strategies to address each of the aforementioned factors, as well as discuss five main strategy dilemmas that educators might encounter. These strategy dilemmas include: (a) use of grades or marks, (b) use of number of posting guideline and posting deadlines, (c) use of message labels or sentence openers (online scaffolds), (d) extending the duration of the online discussion, and (e) instructor-facilitation. Strategy dilemmas refer to those strategies where previous empirical research shows mixed results when they are implemented. Acknowledging the dilemmas is essential for educators and researchers to make informed decisions about the discussion strategies they are considering implementing.

The third section is a series of studies based on our research over the past 12 years. In this section we review ten empirical studies that examine peer facilitation, and how peer facilitation could promote the following three major outcomes: (a) increase students' online contribution rate, (b) sustain students' online discussion, and (c) foster higher levels of knowledge construction. Using students as peer facilitators may be an alternative solution to educators who wish to avoid the instructor-facilitation dilemma. In this section of the book we summarize these case studies and highlight the major findings. We believe that these findings would be useful to other educators and researchers who are similarly interested in using peer facilitation in their asynchronous online discussion environments.

Nevertheless, it is important to note that peer facilitation should not be viewed as a "cure-all" or panacea for the issues and challenges that online discussion presents. With this in mind, we discuss certain situations that may best be addressed using peer or instructor facilitation in Chap. 8. Three major situations in which students wanted the instructor to act as the facilitator were identified: (a) when the discussion needed to be kept on track, (b) when conflicts arose in the discussion and needed resolution, and (c) when the topic of discussion was new or profound and required expert knowledge.

On the other hand, we also discovered four situations or reasons why students preferred peer facilitation over instructor facilitation: (a) participants feel more at ease in voicing their views in a peer-facilitated setting, (b) participants take greater ownership of the discussion, (c) participants are able to have practical hands-on experience of facilitating a discussion, and (d) peer facilitation allowed participants to reflect deeper on other students' ideas that came up in the discussions.

In Chap. 9, we examine the use of asynchronous voice or audio discussion. So far, most of the discussions in previous research center on text-based discussion. The use of text-based discussion could pose a significant challenge for participants who are weak in reading or writing. Participants also run a higher risk of being misunderstood in text discussion due to the lack of verbal cues. We have been exploring the use of asynchronous audio discussion in the past 2 years and in Chap. 9, we report our findings from two recently conducted studies that examine: (a) students' perceived benefits of using audio discussions, (b) their actual preferred mode of discussion (audio- or text-based) if given a choice, and (c) the levels of knowledge construction exhibited by students who participated in the text-based discussion versus students who used the audio-based discussion.

Finally in the conclusion, we suggest several future research directions concerning the use of asynchronous online discussion in education contexts. These directions include: (a) examining the use of peer facilitation in different contexts, (b) investigating the possible solutions to overcome the strategy dilemmas, and (c) studying the use of online discussion on mobile devices such as pocket PC and smart phones.

Contents

Chapter 1
Introduction

1.1 Introduction

In the traditional learning paradigm, the notion of schooling primarily hinges on the idea of transmitting a certain knowledge base to individual learners (Roehler and Cantlon 1997). Under this educational paradigm, the main task of an instructor was to provide learners with knowledge, while the learners' goal was to learn by individually digesting and organizing the information received (Hsu et al. 2000). Learning is assumed to have occurred when the individuals are able to recall the knowledge presented by the instructor (Hsu et al. 2000).

However, contemporary discussions of education in the recent years are increasingly emphasizing the social nature of learning, or the social constructivist paradigm (Palincsar and Herrenkohl 2002). This does not mean that traditional learning is no longer relevant or useful but that during social learning, the interaction or discussion among students could generate extra activities (e.g., explanation, disagreement) as well as additional cognitive mechanisms (e.g., knowledge elicitation and sharing) which may not occur as frequently in traditional, individual learning (Dillenbourg 1999). So concomitant with an increased interest in the role of interaction in academic engagement and learning, and inspired by the growing body of scholarly work (e.g., Brown and Campione 1994; Brown and Duguid 2000; Resnick et al. 1991; Ruhleder et al. 1996; Vygotsky 1978), educators today are particularly interested in fostering learning environments that provide opportunities for learners to exchange ideas with one another. An example of this would be collaborative learning (van Drie et al. 2005).

Collaborative learning emphasizes the negotiation of meaning or ideas among participants pertaining to the specific task at hand (Dillenbourg 1999; Palincsar and Herrenkohl 2002; Roschelle 1992; Roschelle and Teasley 1995; Stahl et al. 2006). Negotiation of meaning or ideas includes exploring dissonance among ideas or concepts, and suggesting areas of agreement where conflict exists in order to establish a shared understanding (Gunawardena et al. 1997). Through the process of negotiating meaning, participants could broaden their own understanding and

K. F. Hew and W. S. Cheung, *Student Participation in Online Discussions*,
DOI: 10.1007/978-1-4614-2370-6_1, © Springer Science+Business Media, New York 2012

perspective, which is then individually reconstructed into their own long-term memory catalyzed by the individual's prior knowledge and experience (Wu 2003).

1.2 The Role of Discussion

Central to the idea of collaborative learning is the notion of discussion. A discussion provides a platform for students to exchange opinions, share multiple perspectives, and clarify various thoughts (Dunlap 2005). Discussions can also help students increase their awareness and tolerance towards ambiguity, and also help them to appreciate diversity more (Brookfield and Preskill 2005). Student discussion has been identified as one of the activities that students found most beneficial to their learning (Ertmer et al. 2007; Richardson and Swan 2003). Traditionally, discussion occurs in face-to-face learning environments such as a classroom or a laboratory. Such face-to-face classroom discussions, however, are typically limited by several factors.

First, face-to-face classroom discussion usually involves instructor–student interaction, characterized by the Initiate-Respond-Evaluate (IRE) structure (Ng 2011). In IRE interactions, the instructor typically initiates a topic with a question, followed by the students answering the question, and finally an evaluative response (e.g., correct or wrong feedback) from the instructor. The number of questions student ask in face-to-face classroom settings is low (Graesser and Person 1994). Students may not have many opportunities to interact with one another in an IRE-enabled class (Almasi 1996).

Second, face-to-face classroom discussion is limited by the school time-tabling structure. For example, Becker (2000), in a survey of more than 4,000 teachers in over 1,100 schools in the United States found that most secondary students have a continuous block of less than one hour's duration to do work in any one class. The imposition of a time table structure limits the amount of discussion students can have in a class. Although students may continue their discussion outside class time, it is difficult, if not impossible, to get everyone to stay back after school on a regular basis (Lim et al. 2011).

Third, face-to-face classroom discussions are usually dominated by a few students. These students are typically the more knowledgeable, or outspoken ones. In addition, some students feel uncomfortable as they find it difficult to keep up in terms of contributing in a fast-paced face-to-face discussion. Often, by the time they think of a response to a question, another student has already answered, or the discussion has moved on to other topics (Rollag 2010). In this way, students who are shy, quiet, or those who need more time to think before answering, often end up taking the backseat in face-to-face discussions.

The use of computer-mediated communication (CMC) tools may help overcome these limitations. CMC tools enable students to continue their discussion outside their class time, as well as provide opportunities for quiet or shy students to voice their opinions. CMC tools also allow students to have more control over the discussion, as compared to face-to-face discussions which may be dominated by their instructors (Althaus 1997; Jones et al. 2006; Salmon 2004). Despite the many different types of CMC tools, they can be broadly grouped under either the synchronous or asynchronous discussion categories. Synchronous discussion tools such as Microsoft Network (MSN) chat require students to simultaneously log on to the platform in order to interact with one another. Asynchronous communication, on the other hand, does not require students to log on at the same time to communicate with one another.

1.3 Asynchronous Online Discussion

Just what exactly is asynchronous online discussion? The main defining characteristic of an asynchronous online discussion is that the discourse that takes place within it is not real time. This time independent nature of asynchronous online discussion makes it particularly well received by many educators (Hew et al. 2010b; Romiszowski and Mason 2004). Individuals can view the messages many times and long after the messages have been posted and respond to the messages posted at any time they prefer. According to Kearsley (2000), asynchronous online discussion is the second most commonly used capability for online teaching and learning after email. There are currently many software packages that offer platforms for asynchronous online discussions. These include *BlackBoard*, an integrated online delivery and management system for faculty members and students to use, as well as *Yahoo Group, Google Group,* and *Knowledge Forum*, among others.

Unlike synchronous chats, notes or messages posted in an asynchronous online discussion are usually threaded. A discussion thread is a series of messages that have been posted as replies to one another, in a chain. By reading each message in order, a participant or facilitator can follow the conversation easily as it progresses. A single simple discussion thread may remain a straight line or turn into a tree as participants post follow-up messages to replies. The visual display of the threads allows participants to easily view the desired message and post their replies. Figure 1.1 provides a prototypical illustration of possible discussion threads. In Fig. 1.1, Subtopic 1 is an example of a discussion thread. Another example is Subtopic 2.

1.3.1 Potential Benefits of Asynchronous Online Discussion

A review of the literature shows several reasons for the widespread use of asynchronous online discussion in education contexts. Perhaps, the greatest advantage of using asynchronous online discussion is that it allows students to participate in the discussion at a pace that they are comfortable with. The benefit of being able to

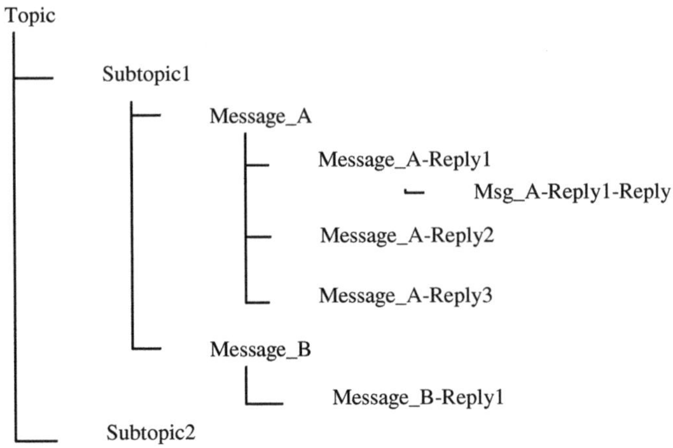

Fig. 1.1 A prototypical illustration of discussion threads

contribute to the discussion at one's own pace is that it gives students ample time to respond to other students' comments (Murphy and Coleman 2004). Such time-delayed interaction could help students develop thinking skills, and solve ill-structured problems (Hew and Knapczyk 2007).

Additionally, all asynchronous online discussion environments require participants to reify or explicitly express what is on their mind (e.g., ideas) as concrete thoughts (e.g., messages) in a forum. These ideas can then be worked on and improved through acts of social interaction, such as questioning, clarifying, or elaborating. Asynchronous online discussion has been referred to as a powerful tool for collaborative learning that "promotes a level of reflective interaction often lacking in a face-to-face, teacher centered classroom" (Rovai and Jordan 2004, p. 3). Some researchers also suggest that the very process of expression could help participants to construct their thoughts more carefully (Vonderwell 2003), and also hone higher level learning skills such as analysis, synthesis, and evaluation (Newman et al. 1997).

There are many ways in which instructors and students could use asynchronous online discussion in actual teaching and learning practice. In the following section, we provide a model of how asynchronous online discussion can be integrated into a course.

1.3.2 An Example of How Asynchronous Online Discussion Could be Integrated into Teaching and Learning

We have been using asynchronous online discussion in many various courses ranging from diploma to graduate programs for the past 12 years. Figure 1.2 shows a model of how we integrated asynchronous online discussion in one of our

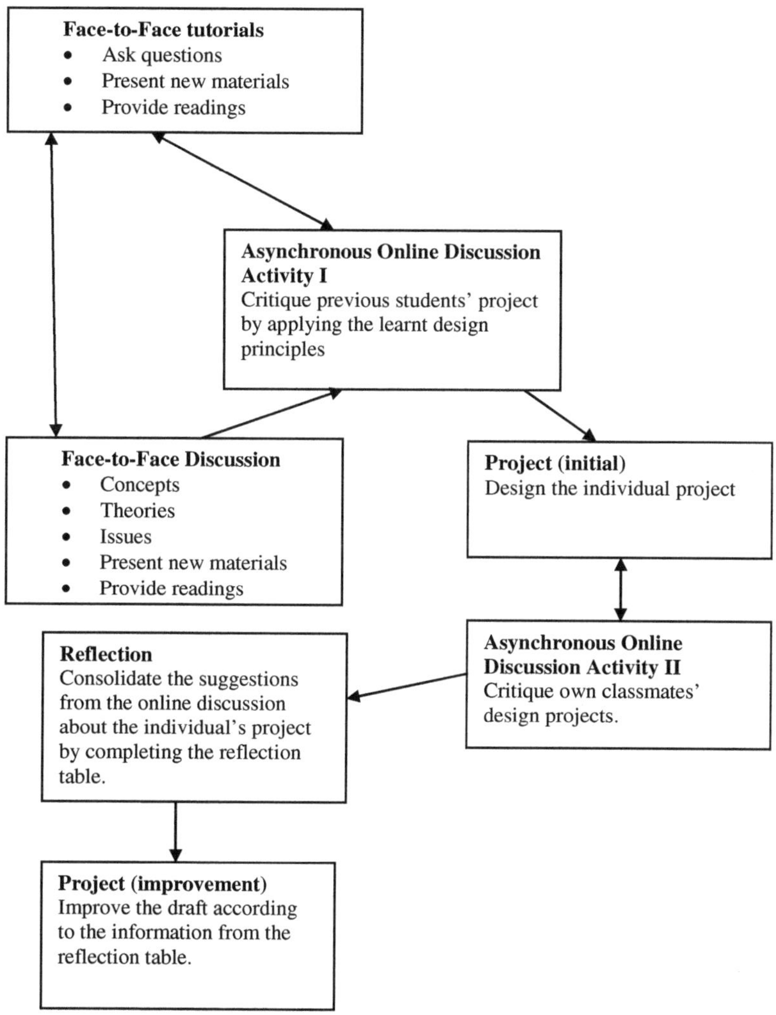

Fig. 1.2 An integration example (adapted from Cheung and Hew 2011, 2010b, 2006)

blended learning courses. Table 1.1 describes the various instructional modes and instructional activities that we used in greater detail. This particular model is based on the revised Bloom's taxonomy which has the following six levels: remembering (recalling information from memory), understanding (constructing meaning from information), applying (using a certain procedure in a given situation), analyzing (breaking material into its constituent elements and determining how the elements relate to one another), evaluating (making judgments based on certain criteria), and creating (putting elements together to form something new) (Anderson and Krathwohl 2001).

Table 1.1 Instructional mode, instructional activities and revised Bloom's Taxonomy (adapted from Cheung and Hew, 2011)

Instructional Mode	Instructional Activities	Revised Bloom's Taxonomy (Anderson and Krathwohl, 2001)
Face-to-Face tutorials	Tutor Asked questions Presented new materials, and led the face-to-face discussion: critique previous student projects	Recalling Understanding Applying Analyzing Evaluating
Asynchronous Online Discussion Activity I	Tutor Led the online discussion – critique previous student projects	Applying Analyzing Evaluating
Project (initial)	Student Drafted their design projects	Creating
Asynchronous Online Discussion Activity II	Student Uploaded their design projects Initiated the online discussion	Applying Analyzing Evaluating
Reflection	Student Completed the reflection tables	Evaluating
Project (improvement)	Student Used the reflection tables to improve their projects	Creating

In this particular integration model, we incorporated two asynchronous discussion activities with face-to-face tutorials, classroom discussions, and a reflection session. In the face-to-face tutorials prior to the face-to-face discussions, the tutor provided students with factual information, concept, and theories about the topic. The didactic instructional approach was typically employed to introduce the topic and highlight some relevant issues with pertinent reading materials (i.e., seed ideas and strategies). Students were also provided relevant reading materials. Conducting face-to-face discussions enabled the students to discuss questions related to the concepts and principles learned with their tutor.

The purpose of the online discussion activity I (critique of previous students' projects) was to find out whether the students had the ability to apply the concepts, theories, and guidelines learned in the critique of other students' projects. Students' identities were kept anonymous in the course of this activity. Essentially, online discussion activity I served as a formative evaluation of students' understanding of the design theories. The tutor was the facilitator of the first online discussion activity. After the first online discussion activity, the tutor may give extra help to students who had misconceptions of the design concepts and theories. Overall, the purpose of these instructional activities (i.e., face-to-face tutorials, online discussion activity I, and extra help for students after the online discussion) was to provide a good foundation for students before they began to design their own projects.

After online discussion activity I had ended, students were asked to create their own projects individually and upload them to their own discussion forums. Students were required to critique their peers' projects on the asynchronous online discussion platform (i.e., online discussion activity II). The purpose of online discussion II was to allow students to discuss problems, solutions, and issues related to their own project, as well as their peers' projects. The students acted as the facilitators for their own forums, and students were encouraged to get feedback from their peers.

After the discussion, each student had to summarize the discussion points in a reflection table (see Table 1.2). Essentially, the purpose of the reflection table was to help each student consolidate the feedback received, and decide how he or she would respond to the suggestions or comments made in the discussion.

Students had to indicate clearly whether they agreed or disagreed with the comments and provide justifications for their decisions. In addition, students had to explain the changes that they intended to make. In short, the reflection table provided the input for students to improve their own project designs.

Overall, a majority of the students found the asynchronous online discussion activities useful and enjoyable because it enabled them to share ideas in their own convenient time, and to examine the viewpoints from all their peers' rather than just the tutor's perspectives (Cheung and Hew, 2011). In addition, no one student dominated the online discussion. We also found that the use of asynchronous online discussion supported two critical ill-structured problem-solving processes (Jonassen, 1997): articulating the problem space, and generating possible problem solutions (Cheung and Hew, 2004).

1.3.3 Participation in Asynchronous Online Discussions

Although asynchronous online discussions may afford certain advantages, such benefits unfortunately can only be enjoyed if students choose to participate in the discussions in the first place (Hew and Cheung 2010b, 2006). Typically, in an asynchronous online discussion environment, a student may participate in the discussion in two major ways—reading and writing messages (Hewitt and Brett, 2007; Lipponen et al. 2003). Reading messages means that the student reads the notes posted by others without contributing any posts to the online discussion (Lipponen et al. 2003). Although individual students could learn by simply reading messages, such an act does not really contribute to or encourage the exchange of ideas in the discussion, because if no postings of messages are made in the first place there will be no messages in the discussion for students to read (Hew and Cheung 2010a).

Participation by writing, on the other hand, requires the student to externalize his thoughts and post the messages in the discussion forum. Bereiter (1994) stressed the importance of externalizing what is in our mind as concrete ideas (e.g., messages) in a discussion forum so that these ideas can be worked on and

Table 1.2 Reflection table with sample students' inputs (extracted from Cheung and Hew, 2011, p. 1329)

	Suggestions made by others	My opinion	Rationale	Changes that I can/will make
1	Teacher shouldn't be present when web activity is done in school lab.	Agree	strongly	Correct project guideline. I mistook that the teacher can be present as long as they are not involved in teaching directly.
I	will remove the presence of the teacher in the lab, in my project report.			
2	Incentives/rewards (stickers etc.) for good work produced (e.g., for creativity; well-thought concepts etc.).	Agree	I found that giving rewards for activities increases motivation amongst students. (from personal experience)	I could indicate that pupils who provide good understanding in their worksheet answers will be rewarded a sticker.
3	Change activity to a revision instead of an introduction to topic (*because the purpose is to help students prepare for the final exams.*)	Disagree	Introduction to topics are a vital part of helping pupils prepare for the final exams as basic concepts learnt in the introduction are also tested.	No changes. I will still keep the web activity to being an introduction to the P5 Science topic of Materials
4	Modify worksheet to include more items in addition to "Cup" to test for suitability of materials (e.g., school bag/ spectacles)	Agree	strongly	By including more appropriate items, pupils are able to clearly understand that more than 1 material can be used to make an item.
I	will include at least another 1–2 items that require more than 1 material to be made from in my worksheet.			
5	Combine with idea suggested in (4.) to conduct cross-subject teaching. - Use Art lesson to allow pupils to create drawings of items with materials indicated.	Agree	Cross-subject teaching, allows total immersion in topic being taught.	I could specify in my closing comments that pupils are given time during their art class to draw out their impression of items being made from unsuitable materials.

improved through social interactions such as questioning, clarifying, or elaboration. In this book, we focus primarily on participation through writing. This is because writing is closely tied with discussion and it can subsume reading, as in the case when a student is replying to an existing discussion message (Guzdial and Turns 2000).

Several researchers (e.g., Davies and Graff 2005; Dennen 2005; Gaspar et al. 2010; Mazzolini and Maddison 2003; Nagel et al. 2009; Palmer et al. 2008; Yukselturk 2010) have suggested that a necessary, if not sufficient, condition for a discussion to aid learning is for students to participate by posting a sizeable number of messages such as comments or questions. For example, Nagel et al. (2009) found a significant difference in the number of posts from students in different grade groups. Nagel et al. (2009) reported that students who failed or abandoned the course posted on average significantly fewer messages in the online discussions than their successful counterparts. On average, the high performing students were active in the discussions and responded to other comments.

The finding of Nagel et al. (2009) study was corroborated by Yukselturk (2010), who found that students' contribution level (i.e., number of post) in a discussion forum was significantly related with student achievement. Palmer et al. (2008) similarly reported that the number of new postings made to the online discussion was significantly related to a student's final unit mark. More recently, Nandi et al. (2011) found that in general, most of the students with higher number of posts achieved distinction or higher distinction grades in the assignments and final assessment. On the other hand, most of the students with few postings either failed or just passed the course. Nandi et al. (2011) concluded that higher achieving students tended to participate in the online discussions more actively than other students did. Gaspar et al. (2010) also found that successful students (i.e., students whose performance in exams exceeded 70 %) tended to contribute more postings, such as questions, that were related to higher cognitive levels indicated in the revised Bloom taxonomy (Anderson and Krathwohl 2001) such as the *analyze* and *evaluate* categories, while failing students posted questions related to lower levels such as *remember* category.

1.3.4 Limited Student Contribution

Unfortunately, students who actively post or contribute in online discussions are usually few in numbers. They are typically the exceptions, rather than the norm. More often than not student contribution in online discussions is limited. In this book, we define limited student contribution as students posting no or few messages, students demonstrating superficial or surface-level critical thinking, or students exhibiting low-level knowledge constructions.

Many previous studies have found that limited student contribution in online discussion forums to be a persistent and widespread problem (Burt et al. 1994; Cheong and Cheung 2008; Cheung and Hew 2004, 2006; De Wever et al. 2006;

Gunawardena et al. 1997; Guzdial 1997; Hew and Cheung 2003a; Hewitt 2005; Hewitt and Teplovs 1999; Jamaludin and Quek 2006; Kanuka and Anderson 1998; Khine et al. 2003; Kucuk et al. 2010; Lazonder et al. 2003; Lee et al. 2011; Maor 2010; McLoughlin and Luca 2000; Nandi et al. 2011; Schellens et al. 2005; Wan and Johnson 1994; Yukselturk 2010).

For example, Guzdial (1997) in his investigation of 18 classes at the Georgia Institute of Technology found that the average thread length was only 2.2 messages, which essentially contained one single message and a response to that message. This is similar to what Henri (1992) referred to as quasi-interaction, which merely involves only two actions: person A communicates with person B and a response from person B. Hewitt and Teplovs (1999) arrived at a similar conclusion after studying the online discussions of seven graduate classes at the University of Toronto. They reported an average thread length of only 2.69 messages. In a later study, Hewitt (2001) found that each student, on average, contributed between two and three messages a week, and that 94 % of the 830 student messages either made no reference to other messages, or only made a reference to one single previous post.

Elsewhere, Wan and Johnson (1994) found that university students contributed less than one message per week; Lee et al. (2011) reported that as many as 50 % of students did not contribute any post; Kucuk et al. (2010) lamented that almost all students (95 %) did not contribute in the online discussion, while Cheung and Hew (2006) reported that many students' discussion ended up a mere question–answer session where participants simply answered their peers' questions instead of taking the discussion to a deeper level.

1.4 The Purpose and Plan of this Book

Why does limited student contribution in asynchronous online discussion occur? How can we alleviate this problem and deal with this challenge? In Chap. 2, we review over 110 empirical studies in order to identify the various reasons or factors leading to limited student contribution in asynchronous online discussion. In Chap. 3, we identify certain empirically based strategies to overcome these limitations. Instructors may use these strategies to increase student contribution, or foster student in-depth critical thinking or higher knowledge construction levels in an online discussion forum. In Chap. 4, we discuss several strategy dilemmas. These are strategies where previous empirical research shows mixed or inconclusive results when they are implemented. Acknowledging these dilemmas is essential for instructors to make informed decisions about the discussion strategies they are considering implementing in the future. In Chaps. 5–7, we report and discuss ten case studies on student or peer facilitation. The use of peer facilitation could provide a possible alternative strategy to alleviate the instructor-facilitation dilemma. In Chap. 8, we discuss certain conditions or situations that may best be addressed using either peer or instructor facilitation. In Chap. 9, we discuss the use of asynchronous audio discussion. Finally, in the conclusion chapter we discuss future research directions concerning the use of online discussion in education context, particularly with respect to mobile learning environments.

References

Almasi, J. F. (1996). A new view of discussion. In L. B. Gambrell & J. F. Almasi (Eds.), *Lively discussions: Fostering engaged reading* (pp. 2–24). Newark: International Reading Association.

Althaus, S. (1997). Computer-mediated communication in the university classroom: An experiment with on-line discussions. *Communication Education, 46*(3), 158–174.

Anderson, L., & Krathwohl, D. (2001). *A taxonomy of learning, teaching and assessing: A revision of Bloom's taxonomy of educational objectives.* New York: Addison Wesley Longman.

Becker, H. J. (2000). Findings from the teaching, learning, and computing survey: Is larry cuban right? *Education Policy Analysis Archives, 8*(51). Retrieved on July 11, 2005 from http://epaa.asu.edu/epaa/v8n51/

Bereiter, C. (1994). Constructivism, socioculturalism, and Popper's World 3. *Educational Researcher, 23*(7), 21–23.

Brookfield, S. D., & Preskill, S. (2005). *Discussion as a way of teaching: Tools and techniques for democratic classrooms* (2nd ed.). San Francisco: Jossey-Bass.

Brown, A. L., & Campione, J. S. (1994). Guided discovery in a community of learners. In K. McGilly (Ed.), *Classroom lessons: Integrating cognitive theory and classroom practice* (pp. 229–272). Cambridge: Massachusetts Institute of Technology Press.

Brown, J. S., & Duguid, P. (2000). *The social life of information.* Boston: Harvard Business School Press.

Burt, M.T., Grady, M. & McMann, G. (1994). *Interaction analysis of an inter-university computer conference.* Paper presented at the Distance Learning Research Conference, College Station, Texas.

Cheung, W. S., & Hew, K. F. (2004). Evaluating the extent of ill-structured problem solving process among pre-service teachers in an asynchronous online discussion and reflection log environment. *Journal of Educational Computing Research, 30*(3), 197–227.

Cheung, W. S., & Hew, K. F. (2006). Examining Students' Creative and Critical Thinking and Student to Student Interactions in An Asynchronous Online Discussion Environment: A Singapore Case Study. *Asia-Pacific Cybereducation Journal*, 2(2). Retrieved June 11, 2010 from http://www.acecjournal.org/current_issue_current_issue.php.

Cheung, W. S., & Hew, K. F. (2011). Design and evaluation of two blended learning approaches: Lessons learned. *Australasian Journal of Educational Technology, 27*(8), 1319–1337.

Davies, J., & Graff, M. (2005). Performance in e-learning: Online participation and student grades. *British Journal of Educational Technology, 36*(4), 657–663.

De Wever, B., Schellens, T., Valcke, M., & Van Keer, H. (2006). Content analysis schemes to analyze transcripts of online asynchronous discussion groups: A review. *Computers & Education, 46*, 6–28.

Dennen, V. P. (2005). From message posting to learning dialogues: Factors affecting learner participation in asynchronous discussion. *Distance Education, 26*(1), 127–148.

Dillenbourg, P. (1999). Introduction: What do you mean by 'collaborative learning?' In P. Dillenbourg (Ed.), *Collaborative learning: Cognitive and computational approaches* (pp. 1–19). Amsterdam: Pergamon Elsevier Science.

Dunlap, J. C. (2005). Workload reduction in online courses: Getting some shuteye. *Performance and Improvement, 44*(5), 18–25.

Ertmer, P. A., Richardson, J. C., Belland, B., Camin, D., Connolly, P., Coulthard, G., et al. (2007). Using peer feedback to enhance the quality of student online postings: An exploratory study. *Journal of Computer Mediated Communication, 12*(2), 412–433. 10.1111/j.1083-6101.2007.00331.x.

Gaspar, A., Langevin, S., Boyer, N., & Armitage, W. (2010). Students' activity focus in online asynchronous peer learning forums. *Informatics in Education, 9*(1), 1–36.

Graesser, A. C., & Person, N. K. (1994). Question asking during tutoring. *American Educational Research Journal, 31*(1), 104–137.

Gunawardena, C. N., Lowe, C. A., & Anderson, T. (1997). Analysis of a global online debate and the development of an interaction analysis model for examining social construction of knowledge in computer conferencing. *Journal Educational Computing Research, 17*(4), 397–431.

Guzdial, M. (1997). Information ecology of collaborations in educational settings: Influence of tool. In R. Hall, N. Miyake, & N. Enyedy (Eds.), *Proceedings of computer-supported collaborative learning* (pp. 83–90). Toronto: Lawrence Erlbaum Associates.

Guzdial, M., & Turns, J. (2000). Effective discussion through a computer-mediated anchored forum. *Journal of the Learning Sciences, 9*(4), 437–469.

Henri, F. (1992). Computer conferencing and content analysis. In A. R. Kaye (Ed.), *Collaborative learning through computer conferencing: The Najaden papers* (pp. 117–136). Berlin: Springer-Verlag.

Hew, K. F., & Cheung, W. S. (2003). Evaluating the participation and quality of thinking of pre-service teachers in an asynchronous online discussion environment: Part I. *International Journal of Instructional Media, 30*(3), 247–262.

Hew, K. F., & Cheung, W. S. (2010a). Possible factors influencing Asian students' degree of participation in peer-facilitated online discussion forums: A case study. *Asia Pacific Journal of Education, 30*(1), 85–104.

Hew, K. F., & Cheung, W. S. (2010b). Fostering higher knowledge construction levels in online discussion forums: An exploratory case study. *International Journal of Web-based Learning and Teaching Technologies, 5*(4), 44–55.

Hew, K. F., & Knapczyk, D. (2007). Analysis of Ill-structured problem solving, mentoring functions, and perceptions of practicum teachers and mentors toward online mentoring in a field-based practicum. *Instructional Science, 35*(1), 1–40.

Hewitt, J. (2001). Beyond threaded discourse. *International Journal of Educational Telecommunications, 7*(3), 207–221.

Hewitt, J. (2005). Toward an understanding of how threads die in asynchronous computer conferences. *Journal of the Learning Sciences, 14*(4), 567–589.

Hewitt, J., & Brett, C. (2007). The relationship between class size and online activity patterns in asynchronous computer conferencing environments. *Computers & Education, 49*(4), 1258–1271.

Hewitt, J., & Teplovs, C. (1999). An analysis of growth patterns in computer conferencing threads. In C. Hoadley & J. Roschelle (Eds.), *Proceedings of the Computer Support for Collaborative Learning (CSCL) 1999 Conference*, Dec. 12–15. Palo Alto, CA: Stanford University.

Hsu, J. F., Chen, D., & Hung, D. (2000). Learning theories and IT: The computer as a tutor. In M. D. Williams (Ed.), *Integrating technology into teaching and learning* (pp. 71–92). Singapore: Prentice-Hall.

Jamaludin, A., & Quek, C. L. (2006). Using asynchronous online discussions in primary school project work. *Australasian Journal of Educational Technology, 22*(1), 64–87.

Jonassen, D. H. (1997). Instructional design models for well-structured and ill-structured problem solving learning outcomes. *Educational Technology Research and Development, 45*(1), 65–94.

Jones, R. H., Garralda, A., Li, D., & Lock, G. (2006). Interactional dynamics in online and face-to-face peer-tutoring sessions for second language writers. *Journal of Second Language Writing, 15*(1), 1–23.

Kanuka, H., & Anderson, T. (1998). Online Social Interchange, Discord, and Knowledge Construction. *The Journal of Distance Education*, 13(1). Retrieved September 30, 2008 from http://www.jofde.ca/index.php/jde/article/view/137/412.

Kearsley, G. (2000). *Online Education: Learning and Teaching in cyberspace*. Belmont: Wadsworth.

Khine, M. S., Yeap, L. L., & Lok, A. T. C. (2003). The quality of message ideas, thinking and interaction in an asynchronous CMC environment. *Educational Media International, 40*(1/2), 115–125.

Kucuk, M., Genc-Kumtepe, E., & Tasci, D. (2010). Support services and learning styles influencing interaction in asynchronous online discussions. *Educational Media International, 47*(1), 39–56.

Lazonder, A. W., Wilhelm, P., & Ootes, A. A. W. (2003). Using sentence openers to foster student interaction in computer-mediated learning environments. *Computers & Education, 41*, 291–308.

Lee, H., Kim, J. W., & Hackney, R. (2011). Knowledge hoarding and user acceptance of online discussion board systems in elearning: A case study. *Computers in Human Behavior, 27*, 1431–1437.

Lim, S. C. R., Cheung, W. S., & Hew, K. F. (2011). Critical thinking in asynchronous online discussion: An investigation of student facilitation techniques. *New Horizons in Education, 59*(1), 52–65.

Lipponen, L., Rahikainen, M., Lallimo, J., & Hakkarainen, K. (2003). Patterns of participation and discourse in elementary students' computer-supported collaborative learning. *Learning and Instruction, 13*(5), 487–509.

Maor, D. (2010). Examining cognitive attributes in student-teacher and student–student online interactions. In *Proceedings of Global Learn Asia Pacific 2010* (pp. 4247–4252). AACE.

Mazzolini, M., & Maddison, S. (2003). Sage, guide or ghost? The effect of instructor intervention on student participation in online discussion forums. *Computers & Education, 40*, 237–253.

McLoughlin, C. & Luca, J. (2000). Cognitive engagement and higher order thinking through computer conferencing: We know why but do we know how? In A. Herrmann and M.M. Kulski (Eds), *Flexible Futures in Tertiary Teaching. Proceedings of the 9th Annual Teaching Learning Forum*, 2–4 February 2000. Perth: Curtin University of Technology. Retrieved on November 7, 2008 from http://lsn.curtin.edu.au/tlf/tlf2000/mcloughlin.html.

Murphy, E., & Coleman, E. (2004). Graduate students' experiences of challenges in online asynchronous discussions. *Canadian Journal of Learning and Technology*, 30(2). Retrieved August 5, 2011 from http://www.cjlt.ca/index.php/cjlt/article/view/128/122.

Nagel, L., Blignaut, A. S., & Cronje, J. C. (2009). Read-only participants: A case for student communication in online courses. *Interactive Learning Environments, 17*(1), 37–51.

Nandi, D., Hamilton, M., Harland, J., & Warburton, G. (2011). How active are students in online discussion forums. In J. Hamer & M. de Raadt. (Eds.), *Proceedings of the 13th Australasian Computing Education Conference* 2011 (Vol. 114, pp. 125–134). Perth, Australia: Australia Computer Society.

Newman, D. R., Johnson, C., Webb, B., & Cochrane, C. (1997). Evaluating the quality of learning in computer supported cooperative learning. *Journal of the American Society of Information Science, 48*, 484–495.

Ng, C. S. L. (2011). *The influence of peer facilitation techniques and other factors on online forum interaction*. Unpublished doctoral dissertation, National Institute of Education, Singapore.

Palincsar, A. S., & Herrenkohl, L. R. (2002). Designing collaborative learning contexts. *Theory into Practice, 41*(1), 26–32.

Palmer, S., Holt, D., & Bray, S. (2008). Does the discussion help? The impact of a formally assessed online discussion on final student results. *British Journal of Educational Technology, 39*(5), 847–858. doi:10.1111/j.1467-8535.2007.00780.x.

Resnick, L. B., Levine, J. M., & Teasley, S. D. (Eds.). (1991). *Perspectives on socially shared cognition*. Washington DC: American Psychological Association.

Richardson, J. C., & Swan, K. (2003). Examining social presence in online courses in relation to students' perceived learning and satisfaction. *Journal of Asynchronous Learning Networks, 7*(1), 68–88.

Roehler, L. R., & Cantlon, D. J. (1997). Scaffolding: A powerful tool in social constructivist classrooms. In K. Hogan & M. Pressley (Eds.), *Scaffolding student learning* (pp. 6–42). Cambridge: Brookline Books.

Rollag, K. (2010). Teaching business cases online through discussion boards: Strategies and best practices. *Journal of Management Education, 34*(4), 499–526.

Romiszowski, A., & Mason, R. (2004). Computer-Mediated Communication. In D. Jonassen (Ed.), *Handbook of Research on Educational Communications and Technology* (pp. 397–431). Mahwah: Lawrence Erlbaum Associates Publishers.

Roschelle, J. (1992). Learning by collaborating: Converging conceptual change. *The Journal of the Learning Sciences, 2*, 235–276.

Roschelle, J., & Teasley, S. (1995). The construction of shared knowledge in collaborative problem solving. In C. O'Malley (Ed.), *Computer-supported collaborative learning* (pp. 69–197). Berlin: Springer Verlag.

Rovai, A. & Jordan, H. (2004). Blended learning and sense of community: a comparative analysis with traditional and fully online graduate courses. *International Review of Research in Open and Distance Learning,* 5, 2. Retrieved January 27, 2012, from http://www.irrodl.org/index.php/irrodl/article/view/192/795.

Ruhleder, K., Jordan, B., & Elmes, M. B. (1996). *Wiring the "new organization": Integrating collaborative technologies and team-based work.* Paper presented at the Annual Meeting of the Academy of Management.

Salmon, G. (2004). *E-moderating: The key to teaching and learning online.* London: Taylor & Francis Group.

Schellens, T., Keer, H. V., & Valcke, M. (2005). The impact of role assignment on knowledge construction in asynchronous discussion groups. *Small Group Research, 36*(6), 704–745.

Stahl, G., Koshmann, T. & Suthers, D.D. (2006). Computer-supported collaborative learning. In R.K.Sawyer, (Ed.), *The Cambridge handbook of sciences* (pp. 409-425). New York: Cambridge University Press.

Van Drie, J., van Boxtel, C., Jaspers, J., & Kanselaar, G. (2005). Effects of representational guidance on domain specific reasoning in CSCL. *Computers in Human Behavior, 21*, 575–602.

Vonderwell, S. (2003). An examination of asynchronous communication experiences and perspectives of students in an online course: A case study. *The Internet and Higher Education, 6*, 77–90.

Vygotsky, L. S. (1978). *Mind in society.* Cambridge, MA: Harvard University Press.

Wan, D., & Johnson, P. M. (1994). Computer supported collaborative learning using CLARE: The approach and experimental findings. In R. Furuta & C. Neuwirth (Eds.), *Proceedings of CSCW'94* (pp. 187–198). Chapel Hill, NC: ACM.

Wu, A. (2003). Supporting electronic discourse: Principles of design from a social constructivist perspective. *Journal of Interactive Learning Research, 14*(2), 167–184.

Yukselturk, E. (2010). An investigation of factors affecting student participation level in an online discussion forum. *The Turkish Online Journal of Educational Technology*, 9(2). Retrieved August 11, 2011 from http://tojet.net/articles/923.pdf.

Chapter 2
Challenges: Findings from Previous Empirical Research

2.1 Sources of Data

A search of the literature was performed across the following six databases: Academic Search Premier, Business Source Premier, Communication and Mass Media Complete, ERIC, Library Information Science and Technology abstracts, and PsyARTICLES. The use of these six databases was deemed reasonable and sufficient because together these databases cover more than 11,000 journals, and have been often used by other scholars in their search for empirical articles (e.g., Hew and Brush 2007; Hew and Cheung 2010b; Luppicini 2007; Rinke 2008; Wang et al. 2008). In addition, Academic Search Premier is considered one of the most prominent databases in academic institutions (Blessinger and Olle 2004).

We limit our search for relevant empirical articles to study examining asynchronous online discussions in K-12 and higher education contexts. Non-educational uses of discussion forums such as political discussions, and patient support groups (e.g., mental health support forum) were excluded. Non-empirical descriptions of online discussion programs, or opinion papers were also discarded. As of end January 2012, our search revealed more than 110 articles. Appendix lists the articles which we included in our review of research. Appendix lists the articles we included in our review of the research literature. These articles are summarized—providing brief details of the authors, year of publication, research method, the purpose of the study, participants, and data sources. Please note that we make no claim that the identified publications represent an exhaustive list.

Next, we applied the constant comparative method (Lincoln and Guba 1985) on these articles: we examined each article to identify the factors leading to limited student contribution, as well as the strategies used to alleviate these factors (if any). The factors and strategies were subsequently grouped into a number of emergent categories. Data analysis continued until the categories were saturated, meaning that subsequent articles confirmed the existing categories, instead of identifying new ones.

K. F. Hew and W. S. Cheung, *Student Participation in Online Discussions*,
DOI: 10.1007/978-1-4614-2370-6_2, © Springer Science+Business Media, New York 2012

Table 2.1 Summary of the factors that limit student contribution

Factors	Studies (representative example)
Not seeing the need for online discussion	Dennen (2005), Fung (2004), Zhao and McDougall (2005), Oliver and Shaw (2003), Xie et al. (2006)
Behavior/practice of instructor or participants (e.g., tone of postings—threatening, pontification on the part of others, lack of peer response, lack of instructor response, single-pass strategy)	Bodzin and Park (2000), (Hew and Cheung 2003b,c), Hew et al. (2005), Hewitt and Teplovs (1999), Hewitt (2003; 2005), Jeong (2004), Oliver and Shaw (2003), Xie et al. (2006), Zhao and McDougall (2005), Zhu (2006).
Personality traits (e.g., low degrees of curiosity, extraversion, agreeableness, openness)	Chen and Caropreso (2004), Khan (2005), Oliver and Shaw (2003)
Difficulty in keeping up with the discussion	Cheung and Hew (2006), Jones et al. (2004), Kear (2001)
Not knowing what to contribute	Fung (2004), Hewitt (2005), Khan (2005)
Lack of critical thinking skills	Hew and Cheung (2003b), Cheung and Hew (2006), Khine et al. (2003)
Being content in merely answering queries (low-level knowledge construction)	Cheung and Hew (2006), Gunawardena et al. (1997), Quek (2010)
Technical aspects (e.g., usability issues)	Hummel et al. (2005b), Murphy and Coleman (2004)
Lack of time	Fung (2004), Hammond (1999), Gerbic (2006)
Risk of being misunderstood	Murphy and Coleman (2004), Yeh and Lahman (2007)

2.2 Factors Leading to Limited Student Contribution

In this section we summarize previous research findings on the factors that could lead or contribute to limited student contribution. Ten main factors were identified: (a) not seeing the need for online discussion, (b) behavior or practice of instructor or participants, (c) personality traits, (d) difficulty in keeping up with the discussion, (e) not knowing what to contribute or the lack of meaningful comments to contribute, (f) the lack of critical thinking skills, (g) being content in merely answering queries, (h) technical aspects, (i) the lack of time, and (j) the risk of being misunderstood. Please note that these factors are not listed in order of priority or importance. The 10 factors described above are elaborated in the following sections and listed in Table 2.1.

2.2.1 Not Seeing the Need for Online Discussion

Previous research suggests that the failure to see the need for an asynchronous online discussion can limit student contribution. For example, students did not find it necessary to log on to a discussion forum and contribute in the online discussion as the students and instructors were already meeting face-to-face four times a week in class (Xie et al. 2006). Students may also feel the discussion topics uninteresting or unattractive and therefore not worthy of discussion (Skinner 2009; Zhao and McDougall 2005). Examples of unsuccessful topics include answers to homework because students have little interest in discussing answers to homework after it is submitted (Guzdial and Turns 2000). Students also find it meaningless to contribute if there is no or little sense of connection between the online discussions and the face-to-face classes (Gerbic 2006). This often happens if what was discussed in the online forums was not applied to, or was in some way linked to the subsequent class activity. Consequently, students do not see the online discussions as being essential to their learning (Hammond 1999), but rather as a work that is done for the sake of itself, its purpose being merely to keep the students occupied for a certain length of time.

In addition, students have little interest in contributing to a discussion if no clear expectations are set, or if no incentives (e.g., grades) are awarded for their contribution (Dennen 2005; Gerbic 2006). For example, Dennen (2005) found that in cases where instructor expectations were not clear, student contribution floundered because students did not know how much they were expected to contribute, or how their messages should look like. The results of Dennen's (2005) study also suggested that when grades were not awarded for the use of and contribution to the discussion forum, many students did not post a single message for the entire semester.

2.2.2 Behavior or Practice of Instructor or Participants

Previous research has also suggested that the behavior or practice of participants (e.g., students, instructors) can limit student contribution in asynchronous online discussion. First, students cease contributing if they receive no immediate response to, or comments on their posts from other students (Arend 2009; Chapman et al. 2008; Cheung and Hew 2004; Feenberg 1987; Jeong 2004; Jeong and Frazier 2008). For example, Cheung and Hew (2004) found that some students procrastinated in responding to other people's questions, resulting in great frustrations for those students who were waiting for replies. The delay caused the students to feel that they were speaking into a vacuum (Feenberg 1987)—that no one was responding to them, and so they see no point in writing messages. Chapman et al. (2008) found that students felt devalued and excluded when they did not receive any responses to their posts. Jeong (2004) found that overall, the response rates declined at a rate of 17 % per day in wait time across all messages. Together, these findings suggest that the longer students wait for a response, the less likely a response will elicit reciprocating responses from other students (Jeong and Frazier 2008).

Second, previous studies also suggest that students stop contributing if they perceive that other students pontificate in the online discussion (e.g., giving their opinions about something as though they know everything about it), or if they feel threatened by other students or if the tone of the discussion becomes too emotional (Hewitt 2005), or rude (Murphy and Coleman 2004).

Third, students may cease to contribute if the instructor does not show interest or involvement, such as giving encouragement or feedback. Xie et al. (2006), for example, reported that students were less motivated to contribute if they perceived little involvement on the part of their instructor in the online discussion.

Fourth, the practice or habit of focusing attention on *unread* messages can unintentionally cause a discussion to cease. Hewitt (2005) found that students on average tended to read messages that they had not read before (these messages were typically marked with an unread flag or set in bold typeface), and largely ignored messages they had previous examined. Describing this approach as a single-pass strategy, Hewitt (2003) found that it could lead to two unexpected and problematic side effects: (a) unintended thread abandonment, (b) unintentional changes in discussion topic.

First, single-pass strategy could cause unintentional thread abandonment because threads that did not contain unread messages were not examined and were easily forgotten. Consequently, discussions that were important could be unintentionally neglected and abandoned. Second, single-pass strategy could also lead to unintentional changes in topic because participants who tend to review the latest unread messages may forget key ideas introduced earlier in the discussion (Hewitt 2001). As a result, important issues or topics may be trivialized unintentionally. For example, Hewitt (2003) reported in his study that instead of persisting with a difficult question such as ("What is the role of computer technology in schools", p. 40), participants ended up reflecting on the decision to allow children playing games during school recess.

2.2.3 Student Personality Traits

Students' personality traits could also affect their contribution in an online discussion. For example, Chen and Caropreso (2004) explored the influence of three personality traits in 70 undergraduates majoring in educational psychology on their online discussion participation rates. The three personality traits investigated were: (a)extraversion—a tendency to seek out and engage in social interactions, (b) agreeableness—reflecting the quality of continuing interaction, and (c) openness—reflecting an interest in intellectual and imaginative experiences. Students scoring at or above the 67th percentile of the sample on the three traits were identified as "high", and those scoring at or below the 33rd percentile were classified as "low". High-profile students include those who are sociable, friendly, helpful, and broad-minded; low-profile students include those who are withdrawn, selfish, uncooperative, and conventional. Chen and Caropreso (2004) reported that students in the low-profile group tended to post (one-way) messages that discouraged replies or contributions from other students. Furthermore, these messages were totally unrelated, or at best only marginally related to the discussion topics.

2.2.4 *Difficulty in Keeping Up with the Discussion*

An asynchronous online discussion allows multiple conversations, where a student can interact with more than one student at the same time. However, such an attribute can also create confusion among students, especially if the discussions are diverse and robust. Students, for example, may find it difficult to keep track of the multiple threads of discussion in the asynchronous online discussion. This is because some students might post to a wrong thread, or introduce various different ideas in a single posting. In the latter situation, if other students respond to each of these various different ideas in the same posting, it is likely that one or more of the ideas will spawn various subdiscussions which, if pursued, can veer sharply off-course and develop in a radically different direction as the initial discussion topic. In such cases, it then becomes increasingly difficult to manage and keep up with these numerous subdiscussions (Winiecki and Chyung, 1998) and as a result, the entire discussion breaks down—it becomes incoherent and eventually student contribution ceases (Thomas 2002).

Another reason for the difficulty in keeping up with the discussion is due to information overload on the part of the students. Information overload usually occurs when there is a high frequency of postings, so that individuals are unable to process them and respond adequately (Whittaker et al. 1998). For example, Jones et al. (2004) found that individuals are more likely to end contribution if information overload occurs. Ng and Cheung (2007) reported that participants found it tiring to read many messages. Chen et al. (2012) similarly found that students who encountered information overload tended to post less in the online discussions.

2.2.5 *Not Knowing What to Contribute/Lack of Worthwhile Comments to Contribute*

Limited student contribution in asynchronous online discussions may also be due to students being at loss of what to contribute or having a lack of constructive comments to contribute (e.g., Arend 2009; Chapman et al. 2008; Fung 2004; Dennen 2005; Guzdial and Turns 2000; Khan 2005). Guzdial and Turns (2000) suggested that students may experience a writer's block, in the same way that an empty word processing document may be intimidating to a green writer.

The problem of students having difficulty in knowing what to contribute was also due to the use of discussion problems or questions that called for a single, fact-based answer. This is because there really is no need for further contribution from the other students after a student responds correctly (Dennen 2005; Nandi et al. 2011). Insisting on student contribution will only result in messages that sound alike to one another. For example, Arend (2009) found that students disliked online posts that were repetitions of one another, because the discussion became very limited, being close-ended and having only one distinct solution. Hence, students found it very difficult to find anything new to say.

2.2.6 Exhibiting Surface-Level/Lower Order Critical Thinking

Critical thinking has received considerable attention over the past several years. Critical thinking may be defined as the ability to evaluate the reasonableness of ideas in order to decide what to believe or do (Schafersman 1991; Swartz and Parks 1994). Critical thinking is considered important to students because it allows them "to deal effectively with social, scientific and practical problems" (Shakirova 2007, p. 42). In short, students who possess the ability to think critically will be able to solve problems in an effective manner (Lim et al. 2011).

Critical thinking may be categorized according to a dichotomy of surface- or low- versus in-depth, deep-, or high-level information processing (Bradley et al. 2008; Cheung and Hew 2006; Henri 1992; Newman et al. 1995). Various content analysis models or schemes have been formulated to measure and evaluate this dichotomy of critical thinking. For example, Newman et al. (1995) developed a content analysis scheme to measure critical thinking based on 10 categories: relevance, importance, novelty, outside knowledge, ambiguities, linking ideas, justification, critical assessment, practical utility, and width of understanding. For each category, a number of positive and negative indicators are provided. For example, a positive indicator of relevance (R^+) is "relevant statements", while a negative indicator (R^-) would be "irrelevant statements, diversions". A critical thinking ratio is then calculated for each critical thinking category: $x = (x^+ - x^-)/(x^+ + x^-)$, where x represents the critical thinking category (e.g., relevance, importance, novelty, and so on), with a minimum of -1 for all uncritical thinking, all surface-level and a maximum of +1 for all critical thinking, and all deep-level.

Another content analysis model is that formulated by Cheung and Hew (2006). The researchers created a framework to assess 38 university students' quality of critical thinking by leveraging on and synthesizing the best features of work done by Henri (1992), Swartz and Parks (1994) and Newman et al. (1995). Surface level critical thinking includes: (a) making conclusions or judgments without offering justification; (b) sticking to prejudices or assumptions (such as forming an irrational attitude of dislike against an individual, a group, or their ideas); (c) stating that one shares the conclusions or judgments made by others but without taking the idea further; and (d) failure to state the advantages or disadvantages of a suggestion, conclusion, or judgment.

In-depth level critical thinking, on the other hand, involves: (a) making conclusions or judgments supported by justification; (b) setting out the advantages or disadvantages of a suggestion, conclusion, or judgment; (c) stating that one shares the conclusions or judgments made by others and supporting them with relevant facts, proof, experience, or examples; and (d) making valid assumptions based on the available indicators.

Many previous studies have found that students tend to exhibit surface-level critical thinking in online discussions (Arend 2009; Bradley et al. 2008; Burt et al. 1994; Bullen 1998; Cheong and Cheung, 2008; Hew and Cheung 2003b; Khine et al. 2003).

Cheung and Hew (2006), for example, found that almost half of the thinking exhibited by the students was of surface-level information processing. Most of the surface-level thinking was due to students making conclusions or judgments without offering any justification; proposing solutions with little details or explanations; and stating that one shares the conclusions or judgments made by others without taking these further. Students appeared to regard knowing "what to do" as more important than knowing "why they were doing it".

Arend (2009) sorted an initial list of 60 courses based on student mean scores on the Motivated Strategies for Learning Questionnaire (MSLQ) (Pintrich et al. 1991) that indicated students' self-reported use of critical thinking, as well as instructors' rating of student critical thinking (based on a 7-point scale, 1 = never, 7 = always). Arend (2009) then selected five courses with the highest critical thinking scores and four courses with the lowest. Comparisons between these two groups were made, and the findings were used to yield information about the ways in which online discussions could influence different levels of critical thinking among students. Arend (2009) found that instructors in the lower critical thinking group provided comments that clearly showed their preferred view of an issue, rather than being impartial in their comments. Students were observed to be challenged by the instructor but in a manner where they were directed toward a preferred, correct answer. This led to students changing their thinking pattern and even apologizing for their views that were not consistent with those held by the instructor. Such instructor facilitation failed to foster a conducive environment for higher critical thinking to occur.

2.2.7 Displaying Low-Level Knowledge Construction

One key factor in determining the success of online collaborative learning can be identified through an investigation of the quality of the knowledge constructions that students engage in (Hew and Cheung 2010b). Although there are many different understandings of what knowledge could be, in the context of this book we consider information, procedures, facts, opinions, experiences, or ideas as knowledge. Such a definition is consistent with the notion that emphasizes an applied perspective of knowledge (Hew and Hara 2007a), where knowledge is viewed as information possessed in the mind of individuals related to procedures, facts, concepts, or ideas that can help an individual take action (Alavi and Leider 1999, 2001).

The quality of knowledge construction can be assessed by examining the different levels it occurs. Similar to the case of critical thinking, various content analysis models have been formulated to characterize and measure these different levels of

Table 2.2 A possible comparison between Gunawardena et al.'s (1997) and Garrison et al.'s (2001) models

Gunawardena et al. (1997)	Garrison et al. (2001)
Phase I—sharing and comparing information	Stage 1—triggering event
Phase II—exploration of dissonance, identifying areas of disagreement	Stage 2—exploration of ideas
Phase III—negotiation of meaning	Stage 3—integration of ideas
Phase IV—testing and modification	Stage 4—resolution of dilemma
Phase V—application of ideas, and students' self-reflective statements	

knowledge construction. Two of the most widely used models of online knowledge construction are that of Gunawardena et al. (1997)'s and Garrison et al. (2001)'s.

Gunawardena et al. (1997)'s interaction analysis model was one of the earliest frameworks to characterize knowledge construction during online collaboration. The kinds of knowledge being referred to by Gunawardena et al. (1997) include information, facts, specific examples or experiences, opinions, concepts, or ideas. It describes knowledge construction as having five phases: (a) phase I—sharing and comparing of information, (b) phase II—exploration of dissonance, identifying areas of disagreement, (c) phase III—negotiation of meaning, (d) phase IV—testing and modification, and (e) phase V—application of ideas, and students' self-reflective statement(s) that illustrate their knowledge or opinions have changed. According to Gunawardena et al. (1997), students constructed knowledge by moving from "lower to higher mental functions" (p. 415) where they first share and compare information before negotiating, testing, and applying ideas collaboratively. Thus, phase I may be considered low-level knowledge construction, while phases II–V the higher or advanced levels.

Garrison et al. (2001) proposed that knowledge construction occurs through four stages: (1) Triggering event, (2) Exploration of ideas, (3) Integration of ideas, and (4) Resolution of dilemma. This model suggested that triggering events occur within the shared world of an online learning community, whereas the exploration, integration, and resolution of ideas may occur either privately or collaboratively. In their conception, students construct knowledge by toggling between private reflection and social reflection. According to Koh et al. (2010), Gunawardena et al.'s (1997) model is more oriented toward collaborative knowledge construction, while Garrison et al. (2001)'s model can be used to address both individual and collaborative knowledge construction. However, both models assume that the quality of students' knowledge construction became more advanced in the latter stages. Hence, Garrison et al. (2001)'s stage 1 may be considered low-level knowledge construction, and stages 2–4 the higher or advanced levels (see Table 2.2).

Because constructing knowledge is an endeavor that requires students to reflect and engage in thinking, advocates of asynchronous online discussion suggest that its use can foster high- or advanced-level student knowledge construction discourse due to its allowance for time-independent interaction (Hew and Cheung 2010b).

However, past empirical research suggests that high levels of knowledge construction rarely occur during actual asynchronous online discussions (Garrison 2007; Garrison et al. 2001; Gunawardena et al. 1997; Jamaludin and Quek 2006; Kanuka and Anderson 1998; Liu et al. 2008; Maor 2010; McLoughlin and Luca 2000; Meyer 2003; Osman and Herring 2007; Quek 2010; Vaughan and Garrison 2004).

For example, Cheung and Hew (2006) found that students were more interested in merely voicing their opinions to their classmates' queries—what Gunawardena et al. (1997) referred to as predominantly phase I level of knowledge construction (sharing of information). Consequently, the discussion appeared to resemble a mere question and answer session where students simply answered their course mates' online queries, rather than moving on to higher level knowledge construction such as phases II–V (Cheung and Hew, 2006).

Apparently, this is not an isolated phenomenon. For example, Gunawardena et al.'s (1997) study obtained a result of 93, 2.4, 1.9, 1, and 1.9 % from phase I to V, respectively. Chai and Khine (2006) also used Gunawardena et al.'s model and reported a distribution of 60, 20, 13, 4, and 3 % from phase I to V, respectively. Quek (2010) found that high school students' posts mainly consisted of phase I constructions (82.7 %). Researchers using Garrison et al.'s (2001) model have also concluded that the majority of students' online discussion posts involved the exploration of ideas, while a maximum of 10 % of these posts attained the highest level of resolution (Garrison 2007; Garrison et al. 2001; Kanuka et al. 2007; Meyer 2003; Vaughan and Garrison 2004).

Overall, the results of previous studies suggested that higher levels of knowledge construction such as phases II–V or stages 2–4 are difficult to achieve. McLoughlin and Luca's (2000), p. 5 lament probably summarizes and articulates the problem very well:

Analysis shows that most messages are in the category of comparing and sharing information. There is little evidence of the construction of new knowledge, critical analysis of peer ideas, or instances of negotiations. The discussions do not appear to foster testing and revision of ideas and negotiation of meaning.

These somewhat discouraging results lead naturally to the following question: Why do students tend to exhibit low-level knowledge construction in online discussions? Our review of the literature suggested the following possibilities.

First, the nature of the discussion task or activity that students engage in may influence the levels of knowledge construction. Schellens et al. (2005) found that when the discussion tasks were too complex, the levels of knowledge construction were significantly lower. The researchers suggest that too much complexity (e.g., when the conceptual base of a particular topic or issue is not completely available or made clear to students, or using a foreign language such as English to present information to students who are unfamiliar with the language) could make students feel insecure. They will be at a loss of what to contribute, and lose track of the discussion objective.

Participants' reluctance or hesitance at questioning others' ideas is another barrier to higher level knowledge construction. This can be attributed to two factors. First, participants are reluctant to disagree with their peers because they are not familiar with one another yet. So, they try to avoid posting messages that challenge other individuals' ideas because this may be perceived as being confrontational (Liu et al. 2008). Second, some individuals are rude in their online posts (Hew et al. 2005). Consequently, other participants tend to "play safe", and hold back from critically analyzing viewpoints in order to avoid conflicts in the online discussion.

2.2.8 Technical Aspects

The technical aspects of the asynchronous online discussion software have also been identified as a factor that can limit student contribution (Hammond 1999; Hummel et al. 2005b; Murphy and Coleman 2004). For example, in a study of 20 graduate students, Murphy and Coleman (2004) found that certain limitations of the software design frustrate students who want to contribute their ideas. Examples of these would be the inability to read through discussion postings while composing a message, and the way the software system constantly returns users to the top of the listings when they click to expand a thread: students then have to search through the entire list of postings to find their bearings.

Another technical aspect that limits the contribution of students is the inability to edit and delete messages (Murphy and Coleman 2004). Students were unable to change a posting mistake throughout the entire course, which made them feel uncomfortable and silly. Furthermore, a lot of time and effort is needed on the part of the students to rectify an error in a message—for example, students had to explain their mistake, say what they actually meant to say, re-explain their arguments, and make the necessary correction before someone else responded and made matters even more confusing.

Besides the aforementioned design quirks, technical aspects related to registration and logon can also limit student contribution. Hummel et al. (2005b), for example, found that most students in their study technically did not contribute because they failed to logon to the online discussion system. Specifically, the two-layer architecture of the discussion system without the convenience of a single log-on used by Hummel et al. (2005b) was not transparent to most students. This resulted in students not being able to navigate and find their way to the actual discussion layer.

2.2.9 Lack of Time

Several studies reported that students did not contribute or contributed minimally because they had little time to do so (e.g., Fung 2004; Gerbic 2006; Hammond 1999; Jeong and Frazier 2008; Rollag 2010). Many students attributed their lack of online contribution to other commitments they had such as work or travel schedules. For example, students in Gerbic's (2006) study said that they were under considerable pressure of time as they tried to balance their study with work, and family commitments. Similarly, many participants in Hammond's (1999) study felt that they had too many demands made on them at work and at home to find time to contribute in the online discussions.

2.2.10 Risk of Being Misunderstood

Finally, several researchers (e.g., Yeh and Lahman 2007; Murphy and Coleman 2004) reported that the lack of gestures, vocal, and facial expressions was the greatest barrier that prevented students from contributing to an online discussion forum. This often led to participants misinterpreting others, or being misinterpreted by others in a text-based online discussion forum. Consequently, misunderstandings among various participants are likely to occur and further contribution to the discussion will inevitably cease.

References

Alavi, M., & Leider, D. E. (1999). Knowledge management systems: Issues, challenges, and benefits. *Communications of the Association for Information Systems, 1*(7), 1–37.

Alavi, M., & Leidner, D. E. (2001). Knowledge management and knowledge management systems: Conceptual foundations and research issues. *MIS Quarterly, 25*(1), 107–136.

Arend, B. (2009). Encouraging critical thinking in online threaded discussions. *The Journal of Educators Online, 6*(1). Retrieved February 15, 2012 from http://www.thejeo.com/Archives/Volume6Number1/Arendpaper.pdf.

Blessinger, K., & Olle, M. (2004). Content analysis of the leading general academic databases. *Library Collections, Acquisitions, & Technical Services, 28*, 335–346.

Bodzin, A., & Park, J. (2000). Factors that influence asynchronous discourse with preservice teachers on a public, web-based forum. *Journal of Computing in Teacher Education, 16*(4), 22–30.

Bradley, M. E., Thom, L. R., Hayes, J., & Hay, C. (2008). Ask and you will receive: How question type influences quantity and quality of online discussions. *British Journal of Educational Technology, 39*(5), 888–900.

Bullen, M. (1998). Participation and critical thinking in online university distance education. *Journal of Distance Education, 13*(2). Retrieved February 23, 2012 from http://www.jofde.ca/index.php/jde/article/view/140/394.

Burt, M.T., Grady, M. and McMann, G. (1994). *Interaction analysis of an inter-university computer conference.* Paper presented at the Distance Learning Research Conference, College Station, Texas.

Chai, C. S., & Khine, M. S. (2006). An analysis of interaction and participation patterns in online community. *Educational Technology & Society, 9*(1), 250–261.

Chapman, D. D., Storberg-walker, J., & Stone, S. J. (2008). Hitting reply: A qualitative study to understand student decisions to respond to online discussion postings. *E-Learning, 5*(1), 29–39.

Chen, S.-J., & Caropreso, E. J. (2004). Influence of personality on online discussion. *Journal of Interactive Online Learning, 3*(2). Retrieved July 9, 2007, from http://www.ncolr.org/jiol/issues/index.cfm.

Chen, C.-Y., Pedersen, S., & Murphy, K. L. (2012). The influence of perceived information overload on student participation and knowledge construction in computer-mediated communication. *Information Science, 40*(2), 325–349.

Cheong, C. M., & Cheung, W. S. (2008). Online discussion and critical thinking skills: A case study in a Singapore secondary school. *Australasian Journal of Educational Technology, 24*(5), 556–573.

Cheung, W. S., & Hew, K. F. (2004). Evaluating the extent of ill-structured problem solving process among pre-service teachers in an asynchronous online discussion and reflection log environment. *Journal of Educational Computing Research, 30*(3), 197–227.

Cheung, W. S., & Hew, K. F. (2006). Examining students' creative and critical thinking and student to student interactions in an asynchronous online discussion environment: A singapore case study. *Asia-Pacific Cybereducation Journal, 2*(2). Retrieved June 11, 2010 from http://www.acecjournal.org/current_issue_current_issue.php.

Dennen, V. P. (2005). From message posting to learning dialogues: Factors affecting learner participation in asynchronous discussion. *Distance Education, 26*(1), 127–148.

Feenberg, A. (1987). Computer conferencing and the humanities. *Instructional Science, 16*(2), 169–186.

Fung, Y. Y. H. (2004). Collaborative online learning: Interaction patterns and limiting factors. *Open Learning, 19*(2), 135–149.

Garrison, D. R. (2007). Online community of inquiry review: Social, cognitive, and teaching presence issues. *Journal of Asynchronous Learning Networks, 11*(1), 61–72.

Garrison, D. R., Anderson, T., & Archer, W. (2001). Critical thinking, cognitive presence, and computer conferencing in distance education. *The American Journal of Distance Education, 15*(1), 7–23.

Gerbic, P. (2006). To post or not to post: Undergraduate student perceptions about participating in online discussions. In *Who's learning? Whose technology? Proceedings Ascilite Sydney* 2006. Retrieved January 27, 2012 from http://www.ascilite.org.au/conferences/sydney06/proceeding/pdf_papers/p124.pdf.

Gunawardena, C. N., Lowe, C. A., & Anderson, T. (1997). Analysis of a global online debate and the development of an interaction analysis model for examining social construction of knowledge in computer conferencing. *Journal Educational Computing Research, 17*(4), 397–431.

Guzdial, M., & Turns, J. (2000). Effective discussion through a computer-mediated anchored forum. *Journal of the Learning Sciences, 9*(4), 437–469.

Hammond, M. (1999). Issues associated with participation in on line forums—the case of the communicative learner. *Education and Information Technologies, 4*(4), 353–367.

Henri, F. (1992). Computer conferencing and content analysis. In A. R. Kaye (Ed.), *Collaborative learning through computer conferencing: The Najaden papers* (pp. 117–136). Berlin: Springer-Verlag.

Hew, K. F., & Brush, T. (2007). Integrating technology into K-12 teaching and learning: Current knowledge gaps and recommendations for future research. *Education Technology Research and Development, 55*, 223–252.

Hew, K. F., & Cheung, W. S. (2003a). Evaluating the participation and quality of thinking of pre-service teachers in an asynchronous online discussion environment: Part II. *International Journal of Instructional Media, 30*(4), 355–366.

Hew, K. F., & Cheung, W. S. (2003c). An exploratory study of the use of asynchronous online discussion in hypermedia design. *Journal of Instructional Science & Technology, 6*(1). Retrieved from http://www.usq.edu.au/electpub/e-jist/docs/Vol6_No1/contents2.htm.

Hew, K. F., & Cheung, W. S. (2010). Fostering higher knowledge construction levels in online discussion forums: An exploratory case study. *International Journal of Web-based Learning and Teaching Technologies, 5*(4), 44–55.

Hew, K. F., & Hara, N. (2007). Knowledge sharing in online environments: A qualitative case study. *Journal of the American Society for Information Science and Technology, 59*(14), 2310–2324.

Hew, K. F., Knapczyk, D., & Frey, T. (2005). Electronically training teachers at a distance: What We've learned from an analysis of six different online pedagogical activities. In C. Crawford et al. (Eds.), *Proceedings of Society for Information Technology and Teacher Education International Conference 2005* (pp. 414–419). Chesapeake, VA: AACE.

Hewitt, J. (2001). Beyond threaded discourse. *International Journal of Educational Telecommunications, 7*(3), 207–221.

Hewitt, J. (2003). How habitual online practices affect the development of asynchronous discussion threads. *Journal of Educational Computing Research, 28*(1), 31–45.

Hewitt, J. (2005). Toward an understanding of how threads die in asynchronous computer conferences. *Journal of the Learning Sciences, 14*(4), 567–589.

Hewitt, J., & Teplovs, C. (1999). An analysis of growth patterns in computer conferencing threads. In C. Hoadley & J. Roschelle (Eds.), *Proceedings of the Computer Support for Collaborative Learning (CSCL) 1999 Conference,* December 12–15. Palo Alto, CA: Stanford University.

Hummel, H. G. K., Tattersall, C., Burgos, D., Brouns, F., Kurvers, H., & Koper, R. (2005). Facilitating participation: From the EML web site to the learning network for learning design. *Interactive Learning Environments, 13*(1–2), 55–69.

Jamaludin, A., & Quek, C. L. (2006). Using asynchronous online discussions in primary school project work. *Australasian Journal of Educational Technology, 22*(1), 64–87.

Jeong, A. (2004). The combined effects of response time and message content on growth patterns of discussion threads in computer-supported collaborative argumentation. *Journal of Distance Education, 19*(1), 36–53.

Jeong, A., & Frazier, S. (2008). How day of posting affects growth patterns of asynchronous discussion threads and computer-supported collaborative argumentation. *British Journal of Educational Technology, 39*(5), 875–887.

Jones, Q., Ravid, G., & Rafaeli, S. (2004). Information overload and the message dynamics of online interaction spaces: A theoretical model and empirical exploration. *Information Systems Research, 15*(2), 194–210.

Kanuka, H., & Anderson, T. (1998). Online Social Interchange, Discord, and Knowledge Construction. *The Journal of Distance Education, 13*(1). Retrieved September 30, 2008 from http://www.jofde.ca/index.php/jde/article/view/137/412.

Kanuka, H., Rourke, L., & Laflamme, E. (2007). The influence of instructional methods on the quality of online discussion. *British Journal of Educational Technology, 38*(2), 260–271.

Kear, K. (2001). Following the thread in computer conferences. *Computers & Education, 37*, 81–99.

Khan, S. (2005). Listservs in the college science classroom: Evaluating participation and "richness" in computer-mediated discourse. *Journal of Technology and Teacher Education, 13*(2), 325–351.

Khine, M. S., Yeap, L. L., & Lok, A. T. C. (2003). The quality of message ideas, thinking and interaction in an asynchronous CMC environment. *Educational Media International, 40*(1/2), 115–125.

Koh, J. H. L., Herring, S. C., & Hew, K. F. (2010). Project-based learning and student knowledge construction during asynchronous online discussion. *Internet and Higher Education, 13*, 284–291.

Lim, S. C. R., Cheung, W. S., & Hew, K. F. (2011). Critical thinking in asynchronous online discussion: An investigation of student facilitation techniques. *New Horizons in Education, 59*(1), 52–65.

Lincoln, Y. S., & Guba, E. G. (1985). *Naturalistic inquiry*. Beverly Hills, CA: Sage Publications.

Liu, X., Doore, B. & Li, L. (2008). Scaffolding knowledge co-construction in web-based discussions through message labeling. In K. McFerrin et al. (Eds.), *Proceedings of Society for*

Information Technology and Teacher Education International Conference 2008 (pp. 3041-3046). Chesapeake, VA: AACE.

Luppicini, R. (2007). Review of computer mediated communication research for education. *Instructional Science, 35*, 141–185.

Maor, D. (2010). Examining cognitive attributes in student-teacher and student–student online interactions. In *Proceedings of Global Learn Asia Pacific 2010* (pp. 4247-4252). AACE.

McLoughlin, C. & Luca, J. (2000). Cognitive engagement and higher order thinking through computer conferencing: We know why but do we know how? *In A. Herrmann and M.M. Kulski (Eds.), Flexible Futures in Tertiary Teaching. Proceedings of the 9th Annual Teaching Learning Forum, 2-4 February 2000. Perth: Curtin University of Technology.* Retrieved November 7, 2008 from http://lsn.curtin.edu.au/tlf/tlf2000/mcloughlin.html.

Meyer, K. A. (2003). Face-to-face versus threaded discussions: The role of time and higher-order thinking. *Journal of Asynchronous Learning Networks, 7*(3), 55–65.

Murphy, E., & Coleman, E. (2004). Graduate students' experiences of challenges in online asynchronous discussions. *Canadian Journal of Learning and Technology, 30*(2). Retrieved August 5, 2011 from http://www.cjlt.ca/index.php/cjlt/article/view/128/122.

Nandi, D., Hamilton, M., Harland, J., & Warburton, G. (2011). How active are students in online discussion forums. In J. Hamer & M. de Raadt. (Eds.), *Proceedings of the 13th Australasian Computing Education Conference 2011.*

Newman, D. R., Webb, B., & Cochrane, C. (1995). A content analysis method to measure critical thinking in face-to-face and computer supported group learning. *Interpersonal Computing and Technology, 3*(2), 56–77.

Ng, C. S. L., & Cheung, W. S. (2007). Comparing face to face, tutor led discussion and online discussion in the classroom. *Australasian Journal of Educational Technology, 23*(4), 455–469.

Oliver, M., & Shaw, G. P. (2003). Asynchronous discussion in support of medical education. *Journal of Asynchronous Learning Networks, 7*(1), 56–67.

Osman, G., & Herring, S. C. (2007). Interaction, facilitation, and deep learning in crosscultural chat: A case study. *The Internet and Higher Education, 10*(2), 125–141.

Pintrich, P. R., Smith, D. A. F., Garcia, T., & McKeachie, W. J. (1991). *A manual for the use of the Motivated Strategies for Learning Questionnaire (MSLQ).* Ann Arbor, MI: Regents of the University of Michigan.

Quek, C. L. (2010). Analysing high school students' participation and interaction in an asynchronous online project-based learning environment. *Australasian Journal of Educational Technology, 26*(3), 327–340.

Rinke, C. R. (2008). Understanding teachers' careers: Linking professional life to professional path. *Educational Research Review, 3*, 1–13.

Rollag, K. (2010). Teaching business cases online through discussion boards: Strategies and best practices. *Journal of Management Education, 34*(4), 499–526.

Schafersman, S. D. (1991). *An introduction to critical thinking.* Retrieved August 26, 2011 from http://smartcollegeplanning.org/wp-content/uploads/2010/03/Critical-Thinking.pdf.

Schellens, T., Keer, H. V., & Valcke, M. (2005). The impact of role assignment on knowledge construction in asynchronous discussion groups. *Small Group Research, 36*(6), 704–745.

Shakirova, D. M. (2007). Technology for the shaping of college students' and upper-grade students' critical thinking. *Russian Education & Society, 49*(9), 42–52.

Skinner, E. (2009). Using community development theory to improve student engagement in online discussion: a case study. *ALT-J, Research in Learning Technology, 17*(2), 89–100.

Swartz, R. J., & Parks, S. (1994). *Infusing the teaching of critical and creative thinking into content instruction.* Pacific Grove, CA: A lesson design handbook for the elementary grades. Critical Thinking Press & Software.

Thomas, M. J. W. (2002). Learning within incoherent structures: the space of online discussion forums. *Journal of Computer Assisted Learning, 18*, 351–366.

Vaughan, N., & Garrison, D. R. (2004). Creating cognitive presence in a blended faculty development community. *Internet and Higher Education, 8*, 1–12.

Wang, J., Odell, S. J., & Schwille, S. A. (2008). Effects of teacher induction on beginning teachers' teaching: A critical review of the literature. *Journal of Teacher Education, 59*(2), 132–152.

Whittaker, S., Terveen, L., Hill, W., & Cherny, L. (1998). The dynamics of mass interaction. In *Proceedings of ACM's Conference on Computer Supported Cooperative Work*, (pp. 257–264), Seattle, WA.

Winiecki, D. J., & Chyung, Y. (1998, August). Keeping the thread: helping distance education students and instructors keep track of asynchronous discussions. In *Proceedings of the 14th Annual Conference on Distance Teaching & Learning, 98* (pp. 451-460). Madison, WI: University of Wisconsin-Madison.

Xie, K., DeBacker, T. K., & Ferguson, C. (2006). Extending the traditional classroom through online discussion: The role of student motivation. *Journal of Educational Computing Research, 34*(1), 67–89.

Yeh, H.-T., & Lahman, M. (2007). Pre-service teachers' perceptions of asynchronous online discussion on blackboard. *The Qualitative Report, 12*(4), 680–704.

Zhao, N., & McDougall, D. (2005). Cultural factors affecting Chinese students' participation in asynchronous online learning. In G. Richards (Ed.), *Proceedings of World Conference on E-learning in corporate, government, healthcare, and higher education 2005* (pp. 2723–2729).Chesapeake, VA: AACE.

Zhu, E. (2006). Interaction and cognitive engagement: An analysis of four asynchronous online discussions. *Instructional Science, 34*, 451–480.

References

Chapter 3
Possible Strategies to Overcome Limited Student Contribution: Empirical Findings From Previous Research

Having described the ten factors that can limit student contribution in asynchronous online discussion, we now describe the empirically based strategies to address them in this section (see Table 3.1). The strategies are described in relation to addressing each of the limited student contribution factors. However, before we describe these strategies in greater detail, we provide two general observations about them.

First, it is important to note that at this moment we cannot reasonably establish causal relationships between implementation of the strategies and the successful increase of student contribution in asynchronous online discussions. Many of the studies reviewed were conducted using the descriptive research methodology, without employing control groups. Descriptive research is typically naturalistic and depicts conditions as they exist in a particular setting (Ross and Morrison 1997), rather than determining causal effects. Second, there are several strategy dilemmas, which will be discussed in Chap. 4. By strategy dilemmas, we mean those strategies in which previous empirical research shows mixed results when they are implemented.

Nevertheless, notwithstanding these two limitations, we believe the strategies are still useful. Not only do they offer instructors and researchers informed directions, they also raise issues and present emerging ideas and results in a way that can help readers imagine solutions in their own contexts. At the very least, it is expected that the information presented in this chapter will guide the instructor to analyze problems from more than a single point of view, and possibly suggest solutions that might have otherwise been overlooked.

3.1 Addressing Students Not Seeing the Need for Online Discussion

Five strategies were reported in previous studies. The first strategy is to select discussion topics that directly relate to students' main curriculum (Dennen, 2005; Hummel et al. 2005; Masters and Oberprieler 2004). Student contribution was positively and strongly related to the perceived relevance of the online discussion

K. F. Hew and W. S. Cheung, *Student Participation in Online Discussions*,
DOI: 10.1007/978-1-4614-2370-6_3, © Springer Science+Business Media, New York 2012

Table 3.1 Summary of empirically based strategies

Limited contribution factors	Strategies
Not seeing the need for online discussion	Select discussion topics directly related to students' main curriculum (Guzdial and Turns 2000; Masters and Oberprieler 2004). Make online discussion activity mandatory or give incentives (e.g., grades) for participation (Cifuentes et al. 1997; Dennen 2005; Gilbert and Daggagh 2005; Khan 2005; Oliver and Shaw 2003; Yeh and Buskirk 2005). Also give the online discussion some added value. E.g., post some learning resources such as websites directly related to the main curriculum; however, these resources are not available elsewhere (Hummel et al. 2005a; Oliver and Shaw 2003). Give students clear explanation of the purpose of the online discussion, as well as instructor expectations (Jung et al. 2002; Yeh and Buskirk 2005). Use deadlines or limited time frames for participation (Gilbert and Dabbagh 2005; Kienle and Ritterskamp 2007). Use discussion activities that can directly engage students' personal interests and emotions (Skinner 2009).
Behavior/practice of instructor or other participants (e.g., lack of peer response, lack of instructor response, tone of postings—threatening, pontification on the part of others)	Tutor's involvement in the discussion (Tagg and Dickinson 1995). Use of ground rules (Cheung and Hew 2007).
Personality traits	Combine high- and low-profile students in the same group (Chen and Caropreso 2004)
Feeling lost in the discussion or information overload	Use AOD forums that represent thread links visually to the user rather than representing messages as a list of message headers (Kear 2001; Kear and Heap 2007). Use ground rules to restrict students to post one idea per message posting (Cheung and Hew 2007).
Not knowing what to contribute	Ask open-ended questions where there are no obvious right or wrong answers (Dysthe 2002; Poscente and Fahy 2003). Also pose questions that invite every learner to share their own personal point of view (Dennen 2005; Dysthe 2002). Use sentence openers and message labels such as clarification/elaboration questions, counter arguments, context- or perspective-oriented questions (Choi et al. 2005).

(continued)

Table 3.1 (continued)

Limited contribution factors	Strategies
Exhibiting surface level thinking	Teach and model the use of Socratic questioning to enhance students' critical thinking skills (Yang et al. 2005, 2008). Use of De Bono's six thinking hats (Schellens et al. 2009). Facilitators to build on participants' ideas, by providing their own opinions, as well as new perspectives to examine these ideas. Also use a variety of questions, including Socratic questions, throughout the whole discussion (Hew et al. 2010a). Instructor to take a neutral stance on controversial topics (Arend 2009). Use of anonymity (Cheung et al. 2009).
Exhibiting low level knowledge construction	Use instructor facilitation techniques such as (a) identify areas of agreement/ disagreement, (b) seek to reach consensus (negotiation), (c) encourage, acknowledge, student contributions, (d) focus the discussion on specific issues, and (e) diagnose misconceptions (Lu and Jeng 2006). Assign students the role of summarizer (Schellens et al. 2005). Match discussion tasks to students' available knowledge base (Schellens et al. 2005). Explicitly structure knowledge construction processes to favor the emergence of higher level interactions either through tools such as scripts/coercion or pedagogical models (Beers et al. 2005; Koh et al. 2010).
Technical aspects	Adequate technological preparation (Cifuentes et al. 1997). Use easy navigation functions (Xie et al. 2006).
Lack of time	As of now no clear empirically based strategy is found.
Risk of being misunderstood	Use audio-based discussion (McIntosh et al. 2003).

activity to other course activities and final course outcomes (Dennen 2005). For example, Guzdial and Turns (2000) found that students were more motivated to contribute in the discussion when the discussion topics were tied to the curriculum. Examples of successful topics included exam reviews. More often than not, exam reviews were found to be valuable to students because the online discussion enables students to explore solutions to the reviews and critique other solutions (Guzdial and Turns 2000).

Second, make the online discussion mandatory or give incentives such as grades for student contribution. Giving marks for online contribution is perhaps one of the most widely used strategies. For example, Cifuentes et al. (1997) in their study of 100 preservice teachers found that increasing the weight of online discussion in the final grade provided incentive for students to contribute in the discussion. The increased emphasis on asynchronous online discussion within the grading system appeared to have had a positive effect on student contribution. Yeh and Buskirk (2005) similarly found that including online discussion as part of the grading criteria was found to be the best intervention to enhance student posting. This finding was confirmed again in a later study by Yeh and Lahman (2007) who reported that the majority of students being interviewed indicated that grade was the most important motivator for online posting. Similarly, Cheung and Hew (2005) found that a majority of participated in the online discussion because it was a part of the course requirement, and the instructor awarded marks for it.

Third, give clear explanations of the purpose of the online discussion. For example, Cheung and Hew (2005) found that students who had a more thorough understanding of the purpose of the online discussion contributed their ideas or opinions more frequently than those who did not. If the purpose of the online discussion was not properly understood, students tended to lose interest, and subsequently stop contributing to the discussion. Other researchers have found that instructors' expectations, such as asking students explicitly to share ideas and information, were found to increase student contribution in online discussions (Jung et al. 2002). In addition, instructors should inform students of how many postings (quantitative guidelines) they were expected to contribute to the discussion. Setting up such expectations help encourage students to contribute messages and participate in the online discussion. Students often look to these guidelines as easily recognizable indicators of them meeting the required expectations (Dennen 2001).

Fourth, give posting deadlines for student contribution. Kienle and Ritterskamp (2007), for example, utilized two deadlines and found that student contribution was highest on deadline days, especially in the minutes just before the deadline. This was confirmed by Thomas (2002) who used deadlines clustered around three discussion themes and found that as each deadline for the particular discussion approached, the number of messages posted correspondingly increased.

Fifth, use discussion activities that can directly engage students' personal interests and emotions. According to Skinner (2009), personal interest in a topic is the key that unlocks each individual's motivation to contribute in the discussion.

3.2 Addressing the Behavior of Other Participants

Three strategies to address the behavior of other participants in online discussion were reported in previous empirical studies. The first strategy is to establish ground rules. According to Cheung and Hew (2007), ground rules are prescribed directives that guide students' behavior in asynchronous online discussion. These directives, which are measurable, are typically enforced with consequences for violation of these rules (e.g., censure by the instructor). These ground rules may be categorized into two major categories: (a) ground rules for appropriate behavior in an online discussion setting, and (b) ground rules for contribution in an online discussion setting.

The purpose of setting ground rules for appropriate behavior is to provide a healthy learning environment where participants show mutual respect as they interact with one another, and also to avoid charges of plagiarism. Examples of such rules include: no posting of personal insults or remarks, and no vulgarities allowed. The establishment of a respectful environment has been found to encourage participants to contribute their knowledge, ideas, or opinions in an online discussion (Wasko and Faraj 2000).

The purpose of establishing ground rules for contribution in an online discussion is to preempt problems of procrastination. Examples include requiring students to respond to queries within 24 h, so as to ensure a consistent, ongoing discussion (Cheung and Hew 2007). The implementation of ground rules, such as requiring students to reply within 24–48 h, is consistent with the findings of other researchers who reported that students generally continue to contribute if they receive responses from other participants within such a period. For example, based on the analysis of 4,086 asynchronous online messages from seven graduate-level distance education courses, Hewitt and Teplovs (1999) found that responses posted to a thread within 24 h had a probability (26–68) of eliciting additional responses compared to responses posted after a day of inactivity (18–41) and after 2 days of inactivity (0.12–0.31).

The second strategy is to encourage instructor or tutor involvement in the online discussion (Painter et al. 2003). Tagg and Dickinson (1995), for example, found that student contribution appeared to increase in online discussions when the students perceived a continual instructor involvement, evidenced the following six characteristics: (a) a reasonably prompt response to the initial student contribution (between 3 to 5 days), (b) rapid subsequent response to student contributions (an overall average of 3 days), (c) responses directed mainly to individual students rather than groups, (d) instructor responses that are dispersed throughout the discussion, instead of being clustered together, (e) instructor responds to about half the total number of messages posted by students, and (f) a pattern of individual student-addressed messages that acknowledge an individual's contribution, immediately followed with guiding comments.

3.3 Addressing Personality Traits

To address personality traits of students in online discussion, combine students of different traits in the same group. For example, the results of Chen and Caropreso's (2004) study suggested that when high- and low-profile students were grouped together (see earlier descriptions of high- and low-profile in Sect. 2.2.3), they used more two-way communication and were more focused on instructional issues as compared to students who did not undergo such grouping. Two-way communication involved posting messages that directly invite or encourage replies; thereby, motivating other students to contribute to the discussion as well. In contrast, students in the low-profile group tended to post marginally related or unrelated messages, as well as messages that did not encourage responses from other students, hence causing others to cease contributing.

3.4 Addressing Student Difficulty in Keeping Up With the Discussion

Two strategies targeted at addressing student having difficulty in keeping up with the online discussion were described in previous studies. First, to alleviate the possibility of students introducing various different ideas into a single posting that may later spawn increasingly smaller fragments of subdiscussions, establish, and enforce ground rules specifying that only one idea is to be introduced per posting (Cheung and Hew 2007). This would help reduce the problem of information overload.

Second, to help students contribute postings into correct threads, use discussion forums that represent the thread links visually to students rather than representing messages as a chronological list of message headers (Kear 2001). For example, Kear (2001) found that when a discussion forum fails to show the structure of threads, students often submit unthreaded messages, and other students find it hard to see how the messages fit into the different parallel discussions. This results in a lot of confusion, and it becomes a struggle to keep track of what is going on in the discussion.

Even if the discussion shows the structure of discussion threads as suggested by Kear (2001), several researchers argue that students may still find it difficult to refer to specific posts, especially if the discussion contains many messages (Chanlin et al. 2009; Gao 2011). To date, two different strategies have been explored to alleviate this problem: (a) the use of labeled posts, and (b) the use of a concept-map type of discussion forum.

Chanlin et al. (2009) examined the use of labeled posts, and whether they could increase the number of students responding to others. Each online post was given an ID number, so that students could refer to the ID number when responding to any specific post. An example of a labeled post would be "Posting ID: No. 123," and an example of a response to the particular post would be "Referring to Posting ID No. 123 by Jim." Results showed that students in the labeled posting group posted significantly more than those in the unlabeled posting group. Students felt the use of labeled posts was able to satisfy the need for person-to-person communication better; perhaps by means of referring to the individual author's name. Students also reported that the use of labeled posts gave a sense of continuity to a discussion, because any arguments posted could be specifically referred to and questioned for clarity.

Instead of using labeled posts, Gao (2011) examined if the use of a concept-map type of discussion forum (referred to as a discussion map) would promote the number of online posts as well as the sustainability of the discussion. This discussion map environment was developed in Mindomo (www.mindomo.com), based on the assumption that the connections and relations among online posts should be made more visible. In this particular environment, the discussion question was presented in a bubble at the center of the screen, instead of a thread. Participants could respond to the discussion question and other existing posts by adding subbubbles. Participants could also attach a note to each bubble to write more elaborate posts. A link in the discussion map represented only one type of relationship—a reply to a previous post. Gao (2011) found that the threads in the discussion map contained significantly more posts than those in a traditional threaded forum. However, students did *not* make significantly more *cross-thread* connections in the discussion map than in the threaded forum. One possible explanation was that many cross-thread connections made the discussions confusing to follow, with links appearing all over the discussion map.

3.5 Addressing Students Being at Loss of What to Contribute

Two strategies were reported in previous studies to address the problem of students not knowing what to contribute in online discussions. First, because students may experience a writer's block of sorts and do not know what to contribute, use scaffolds. For example, participants are provided with guidance on how to generate discussion messages such as comments or questions. Choi et al. (2005) used a set of online guides to help participants generate three types of questions—clarification or elaboration questions, counter-arguments, and context- or perspective-oriented questions. Clarification or elaboration questions referred to peer-generated questions seeking additional information to clarify or elaborate on learners' initial ideas. Counter-arguments are understood as peer-generated opinions expressing disagreements with learners' initial ideas. Context- or perspective-oriented questions referred to hypothetical questions that changed critical factors in a given problem situation, or approaching the problems mentioned in the study from different perspectives. Unlike the other two, these hypothetical questions were not aimed at indicating a problem with learners' responses, but rather to stimulate learners to think systemically about the dynamic aspects of the problems beyond the levels of the assigned questions. Results suggested that the online scaffolds served as a starting point that helped students generate questions when they faced difficulty with asking questions. Also, students who received online scaffolds contributed significantly more questions than students who did not receive the scaffolds (Choi et al. 2005).

Another way to provide scaffold to students during online discussions is to use a prescribed set of sentence openers or message labels embedded within the discussion forum. Sentence openers are predefined ways to begin a posting, and are usually followed by additional text that helps to complete the student's thought

(Lazonder et al. 2003; Nussbaum et al. 2002). For example, a student might compose the message "I do not agree that the use of audio would help clarify this specific content of your multimedia presentation" by clicking the opener "I do not agree" and typing in his supplementary text. Other examples of sentence openers include "on the contrary," "I need to understand," "my argument is," "explain why," "give me an example of," "to me this means," "what does…mean?" (Nussbaum et al. 2002). According to Nussbaum et al. (2002), sentence openers appeared to be most useful for students with low degrees of curiosity or assertiveness. Sentence openers encouraged such students to contribute their own thoughts, and to initiate debates in an online discussion environment.

Message labels, on the other hand, are certain classifications that are added to learners' online messages (Ng et al. 2010). In other words, students have to explicitly label each message with a prescribed label, such as "Identify problems" and "Develop Solutions" (Ng et al. 2010). For example, Cho and Jonassen (2002) examined the use of predetermined message types (e.g., data, hypothesis, principle) that reflected ill-structured problem-solving processes in a threaded online discussion environment. Results showed that groups using the scaffold produced significantly more problem-solving communication than groups that did not have access to the scaffold.

Second, instead of using discussion prompts or questions that merely call for a single fact-based answer, use open-ended questions where there may be more than one possible solution, or no obvious right or wrong answers. Asking open-ended questions has been found to encourage student contribution and stimulate students' interactions (Dysthe 2002; Poscente and Fahy 2003). In addition, questions that invite students to share their own point of view from their personal and/or work life (Dysthe 2002; Dennen 2005; Nandi et al. 2011) have also been found useful in increasing student contributions in the discussion. For example, in Dysthe's (2002) study, students were asked to: reflect on an article, present examples which illustrate the point of the article, and explain why these examples were relevant by sharing their own personal opinions.

3.6 Addressing Students' Surface-Level Critical Thinking

To address students' surface-level critical thinking, the current review of the literature has suggested the following strategies. First, to enhance students' critical thinking skills, the instructor or tutor should teach and model the use of Socratic questioning, such as questions of clarification, questions that probe assumptions, questions that probe reasons and evidence, questions about viewpoints or perspectives, questions that probe implications and consequences, and questions about the question (Strang 2011; Yang 2008; Yang et al. 2005; Yang et al. 2008). Table 3.2 shows some possible examples of Socratic questions.

Yang et al. (2005) found that teaching and modeling of Socratic questioning helped students demonstrate a greater depth of critical thinking. The depth of

Table 3.2 Examples of socratic questions (adapted from Salam and Hew 2010)

Category of Socratic question	Examples
Questions about the question	Did I assume the question correctly? Why?
Questions of clarification	What is my main point?
	Could I have put it another way? If yes, how?
Questions that probe assumptions	What am I assuming?
	What could I have assumed instead?
Questions about viewpoints or perspectives	Where did I get the idea that the source is reliable or not reliable or both?
	Is my opinion of the source one-sided? Why
	What would someone who disagrees say?
Questions that probe reason and evidence	What examples/evidence could I provide to support my opinion?
Questions that probe implications and consequences	What could be some possible results of my ideas/ suggestions?
	What are some possible positive or negative outcomes of my ideas/suggestions?

critical thinking skills was measured using a modified Newman et al.(1995)'s coding scheme. Yang et al. (2008) found that if the instructor modeled and challenged students' critical thinking skills at the beginning of the discussion rather than in the middle of the semester, students seemed to be more motivated to contribute. Also, students maintained their critical thinking skills even after the instructor discontinued their facilitation of critical thinking questioning.

Besides the use of Socratic questioning, the instructor may also consider using Edward De Bono (1991) six thinking hats. Schellens et al. (2009) conducted an experiment research to examine the impact of the six thinking hats on student critical thinking. In the experimental condition, students were required to tag their contributions according to De Bono (1991) six thinking hats by means of a computer predefined script (Schellens et al. 2009). Table 3.3 summarizes the six hats utilized in the Schellens et al. (2009) study.

In the control condition, students were engaged in an identical assignment, but were not made to label their online posts. Analyses with regard to the overall comparison of critical thinking showed significantly more positive and less negative indicators of critical thinking per posted message in the experimental condition, as compared to the control condition. The indicators of critical thinking were measured by means of Newman et al. (1995) scheme. More specifically, students in the experimental condition posted significantly more messages related to the critical thinking indicators of *discussion focus* and *novelty*. In other words, students who are required to tag their contributions are more prone to engage in focused and in-depth discussions. They are also more likely to introduce new problem-related information and deal with new ideas, as compared to their peers in the control discussion.

Third, facilitators should also consider using certain techniques. In one of our studies (Hew et al. 2010a), we examined the online discussion forums of a

Table 3.3 Six thinking hats (Schellens et al. 2009, p. 81)

Thinking hats	Descriptions and examples
White hat	White reminds us of paper. The white hat can be used to focus the attention on available information and encloses objective information. E.g., What information do we have? What information do we need?
Blue hat	The blue hat is the color of the sky high above us. This hat stands for reflection, to consider whether the right topic is addressed. E.g., What is relevant? Defining what to think about and deciding what goals are to be reached.
Green hat	The green hat is associated with grass, fertility, and growth. Wearing this hat assumes that one is being creative and cultivating new ideas. E.g., Bringing in new ideas. What are the alternatives and the possibilities?
Black hat	Black is reminiscent of the toga of a judge, and stands for "watch out." This hat points to the pitfalls of possible solutions. Linking ideas together and evaluating the possible solutions. Looking at why this solution will or will not fail.
Yellow hat	The yellow hat is associated with the sun and positivism, and also trying to integrate and apply the solutions. Validating the solutions within the group, giving feedback, and applying the outcome to the context of the real world.
Red hat	The red hat suggests fire and warmth and stands for emotions, intuition, and feelings. Sharing an opinion or an intuition without a clear argumentation.

graduate course. Each student was required to design and develop an instructional software. After the students had drafted their projects, they uploaded the materials into their individual discussion forums. Each student facilitated the discussions in his or her own forum to critique each other's instructional project. At the end of the course, the students' postings were analyzed to determine the quality of critical thinking manifested in the discussions, using the surface- and in-depth level indicators indicated by Cheung and Hew (2006). The top 30 % of forums in terms of the most number of in-depth critical thinking incidences, hereafter, referred to as the higher level group, were identified. Next, the bottom 30 % of forums were identified as the lower level critical thinking group. Our analysis of these two critical thinking groups revealed some important and interesting differences.

First, in the higher level group, the facilitators built on the participants' ideas and suggestions by providing their own opinions, as well as new perspectives to examine these ideas. Participants in the higher level group were also asked to either justify their earlier stand. Such facilitation, however, was missing in the lower level group. The facilitators in the lower level group seemed to take a laissez-faire or indifferent attitude towards the discussion occurring in their forums. Each participant would post a different idea to the same issue or question and no one bothered to further elaborate on the idea or question the idea. Consequently, the ideas in the lower level group forums were not well developed and at times seemed disjointed. Second, facilitators in the higher-level group used a wider variety of questions, including Socratic questioning, and employed them consistently throughout the entire discussion, unlike their counterparts in the lower level groups who posted questions only at the start of the discussion.

Instructors should also remain neutral in their comments. Arend (2009) found that instructors who adopted a neutral stance on controversial topics had greater success in encouraging their students to think more critically about the topics, as well as other perspectives and views. On the other hand, instructors who explicitly shared their personal thoughts on the topics being discussed ran a high risk of closing down students' thinking processes. This is because students often tend to think or assume that the instructors' views are correct.

Finally, instructors may consider using anonymity to encourage students to interact and provide critical feedback. In one of our studies (Cheung et al. 2009), we examined students' level of critical thinking when they were asked to discuss other people's projects. The participants had to complete two online discussion activities. In the first discussion activity, the identities of the project owners were hidden from the participants, whereas in the second discussion activity, students knew the identities of the owners. We found that messages posted in a setting where the identities of object (e.g. projects or assignments) owners were unknown (i.e. anonymous) tended to fall more frequently into the in-depth critical thinking category, as compared to messages posted in a setting where object owners were identified. Overall, our results showed that participants functioned at the in-depth level of critical thinking about 80 % of the time when there was object owner anonymity, as compared to only 54 % when the object owners' identities were revealed. The level of critical thinking was established through the framework formulated by Cheung and Hew (2006).

One legitimate concern instructors may have concerning the use of anonymity is the possible occurrence of aggressive and malicious student behavior, such as flaming (Bertera and Littlefield 2003). However, we have found no evidence of this in our study so far (Cheung et al. 2009). We believe that incidences of malicious behavior occur much less frequently in an institutional course-related discussion forum, as compared to public online forums. This is because in an institutional setting, the participants are aware that they are anonymous only to their peers and not to the instructor. This creates a sense of accountability on the part of the participants, and encouraging them to be responsible in their posting of comments.

3.7 Addressing Students' Low-Level Knowledge Construction

First, the design of the discussion task or assignment that students have to complete could influence the levels of knowledge construction. Schellens et al. (2005) found that when the discussion tasks were too complex, the levels of knowledge construction were significantly lower. Schellens et al. (2005) posit that too much complexity (i.e., when the conceptual base of a particular topic or issue is not completely available, or have not been clearly explained to students, or presented using a foreign language to students who are unfamiliar with the language) could make students feel insecure and lose track of the objective of the discussion.

To circumvent this, Schellens et al. (2005) suggested that the task or assignment should be matched to the available knowledge and existing skill levels of students. In addition, the researchers stressed the importance of design tasks that leave sufficient room for discussion.

Schellens et al. (2005) also suggested that students be assigned the role of a summarizer. Their studies indicated that having students take on the specific role of summarizer in an online discussion resulted in significantly higher levels of knowledge construction as compared to having students take on other roles, such as source searcher, theoretician, and moderator. The summarizers were responsible for identifying the different opinions, describing the comments or postings that held similar points of view, as well as indicating any contradictions, and finally drawing some provisional conclusions. Such tasks or activities tend to relate to higher level knowledge construction phases such as phase II (exploration of disagreements) and III (negotiation of meaning) (Gunawardena et al. 1997). Besides the role of a summarizer, Darabi et al. (2011) found that the debate and role-play strategies were also highly associated with the exploration and integration phases of Garrison et al. (2001) model. These two phases can be considered to correspond to phases II, III, and IV (testing and modification of ideas) of Gunawardena et al. (1997).

In addition, there are other facilitation approaches used by instructors that have been found to be helpful for enhancing knowledge construction in the discussion forum (Lu and Jeng 2006). These approaches include (a) identifying areas of agreement/disagreement, (b) seeking to reach consensus/understanding, (c) encouraging and acknowledging student contributions, (d) focusing the discussion on specific issues, and (e) diagnosing misconceptions.

Other researchers have explicitly structured knowledge construction processes using either tools or pedagogical models in order to favor the emergence of higher level interactions. Beers et al. (2005), for example, examined the use of an ICT-tool to support knowledge construction in collaborative learning environments. This tool uses formalisms which are "constraints that structure conversation and discourse with the aim to guide the exchange of knowledge" (p. 624).This tool coerces the participants into exploring each other's viewpoints in order to explicitly facilitate the negotiation of meaning (example of a higher level knowledge construction, i.e., phase III according to Gunawardena et al. 1997). The function of this tool is similar to that of an online script, such as a sentence opener that models a specific type of dialog. Results suggested coercion was correlated with negotiation of meaning; the more coercion, the more participants would engage in negotiating the meaning of online posts.

With regards to pedagogical models, Koh et al. (2010) investigated the use of online project-based learning and the ways in which it might foster higher knowledge construction levels among students in asynchronous discussions. Specifically, the following three practices of project-based learning should be considered. The first is to assign students an appropriately chosen design problem that is open-ended and complex enough to illustrate iterative design-feedback-refinement cycles. Second, instructors should structure project milestones in an explicit way that guides students to progress from the lower to higher knowledge construction levels (e.g., from idea exploration to problem solutions). Third, instructors should also have students articulate their ideas through artifacts (e.g. paper prototypes and computer prototypes), rather than merely describing the ideas in online posts. Artifacts are useful in helping students externalize their current state of knowledge, and also stimulate feedback and critique. Students would then be more likely to respond in the form of higher knowledge levels as they attempt to justify and reconsider their design prepositions (Koh et al. 2010).

3.8 Addressing Technical Aspects

To address the technical aspects of online discussion systems, two strategies were reported in previous empirical studies. First, ensure that students are equipped with adequate technical skills to use the asynchronous online discussion system. Cifuentes et al. (1997) found that the all-encompassing requirement for a successful asynchronous online discussion is adequate technological preparation on the part of the students, which includes knowing how to set a password, access the discussions, and post messages successfully. Certain facilitator interventions, such as providing students with written instructions and giving face-to-face demonstrations of how to access the online discussion systems, were found to be effective in overcoming the technical difficulties that students faced. Second, use asynchronous discussion systems that have user-friendly navigation functions. For example, Xie et al. (2006) found that discussion boards with user-friendly navigation functions were reported to have increased students' interest and willingness in contributing to the online discussion.

3.9 Addressing the Problem of Lack of Time

As of now, we could not find any clear empirically based strategy on how to address this particular issue. Yeh and Lahman (2007) suggested that instructors have a longer duration of online discussion activity in order to alleviate the lack of time problem faced by students. This is premised on the notion that a longer time allowance would give students more time to think and contribute in an online discussion. This notion is echoed by Jeong and Frazier (2008), who recommended that online discussions be conducted over longer periods of time, so as to allow students who require flexible work or study schedules to contribute as well, and at timings that are convenient for them. Such suggestions and recommendations, however, are often made without the support of any empirical finding. We will discuss this issue in further detail in Chap. 4.

3.10 Addressing the Risk of Being Misunderstood

Finally, to address the risk of student being misunderstood in a text-based environment, we recommend using a voice- or audio-based discussion. Girasoli and Hannafin (2008) suggested that audio-based asynchronous discussion could allow students to speak more coherently and understandably, aided by the use of inflections and expressions that are absent in text-based discussion. The use of tonal cues such as inflections and expressions could potentially help the receiver to better understand a sender's message. In this way, the risk of misunderstanding can be reduced.

So far, there has been little research that examined the use of asynchronous audio discussion (Yaneske and Oates 2010). Some of the existing published research studies include Chang (2010), Gleason (2011), Marriott and Hiscock (2002), McIntosh et al. (2003), and Yaneske and Oates (2010). Yaneske and Oates (2010), for example, evaluated the use of a Wimba Voice Board to support an asynchronous audio discussion. Eleven students in a Master of Arts language learning module participated in the study. Students first learned the principles for selecting or creating podcasts; then designed tasks with reference to the podcasts to support language learning. Students uploaded their designed tasks to the Wimba Voice Board to be shared with their peers and tutor. Students were required to use the Voice Board to give feedback on at least two of their peers' work. In addition, the Voice Board was also used by the tutor to provide feedback on students' work.

Results from the student questionnaire and interviews suggested that the use of voice communication in an asynchronous online environment had several advantages, including increased personalization, the chance to practice one's speaking and listening skills, and an increased sense of understanding. An increased sense of understanding is due to the ability to hear the tone of the speaker. This helps a participant understand a sender's message better and hence lowers the occurrence of misunderstandings. However, some students were inhibited by feelings of embarrassment at hearing their own voice, and by their inability to skim through the audio files quickly. In other words, when the students could not catch a part of the audio recording, or wished to repeat a short section of the recording again, they had to replay the audio message from the start, over and over.

Investigating the role of audio-based asynchronous discussion is also the thrust of our research program. In Chap. 9, we discuss several limitations concerning the existing research on asynchronous audio discussion. We also report two studies which we recently conducted that examined students' perceived benefits of using audio discussions, their actual preferred mode of online discussion (audio- or text-based) if given a choice, and the levels of knowledge construction exhibited by students who participated in the text-based discussion versus students who used the audio-based discussion.

References

Arend, B. (2009). Encouraging critical thinking in online threaded discussions. *The Journal of Educators Online*, 6(1). Retrieved February 15, 2012 from http://www.thejeo.com/Archives/Volume6Number1/Arendpaper.pdf.

Beers, P. J., Boshuizen, H. P. A., Kirschner, P. A., & Gijselaers, W. H. (2005). Computer support for knowledge construction in collaborative learning environments. *Computers in Human Behavior, 21*, 623–643.

Bertera, E. M., & Littlefield, M. B. (2003). Evaluation of electronic discussion forums in social work diversity education: A comparison of anonymous and identified participation. *Journal of Technology in Human Services, 21*(4), 53–71.

Chang, C.-K. (2010). Acceptability of an asynchronous learning forum on mobile devices. *Behavior and Information Technology, 29*(1), 23–33.

Chanlin, L.-J., Chen, Y.-T., & Chan, K.-C. (2009). Labeled postings for asynchronous interaction. *AACE Journal, 17*(4), 317–332.

Chen, S.-J., & Caropreso, E. J. (2004). Influence of personality on online discussion. *Journal of Interactive Online Learning*, 3(2). Retrieved July 9, 2007 from http://www.ncolr.org/jiol/issues/index.cfm.

Cheung, W. S., & Hew, K. F. (2005). Factors affecting learners' satisfaction on the use of asynchronous online discussion in a hypermedia design environment. *Journal of Southeast Asian Education*, 5(1&2), 56–70.

Cheung, W. S., & Hew, K. F. (2006). Examining students' creative and critical thinking and student to student interactions in an asynchronous online discussion environment: A singapore case study. *Asia-Pacific Cybereducation Journal*, 2(2). Retrieved June 11, 2010 from http://www.acecjournal.org/current_issue_current_issue.php.

Cheung, W., & Hew, K. (2007). Use of Ground Rules and Guidelines in Online Discussion: A Case Study. In C. Montgomerie and J. Seale (Eds.), *Proceedings of World Conference on Educational Multimedia, Hypermedia and Telecommunications 2007* (pp. 2753–2758). Chesapeake, VA: AACE.

Cheung, W. S., Hew, K. F., & Foo, A. (2009). Examining the impact of object owners' anonymity on learners' participation rate and critical thinking in an asynchronous online discussion environment. In L. Cameron and J. Dalziel (Eds.), *Proceedings of the 4th International LAMS and Learning Design Conference* (pp. 48-53). Sydney, Australia: LAMS Foundation.

Cho, K.-L., & Jonassen, D. H. (2002). The effects of argumentation scaffolds on argumentation and problem solving. *Educational Technology Research and Development, 50*(3), 5–22.

Choi, I., Land, S. M., & Turgeon, A. J. (2005). Scaffolding peer-questioning strategies to facilitate metacognition during online small group discussion. *Instructional Science, 33*, 483–511.

Cifuentes, L., Murphy, K. L., Segur, R., & Kodali, S. (1997). Design considerations for computer conferences. *Journal of Research on Computing in Education, 30*(2), 177–201.

Darabi, A., Arrastia, M. C., Nelson, D. W., Cornille, T., & Liang, X. (2011). Cognitive presence in asynchronous online learning: A comparison of four discussion strategies. *Journal of Computer Assisted Learning, 27*, 216–227.

De Bono, E. (1991). *Six thinking hats for schools: resource book for adult educators*. Logan: USA Perfection Learning.

Dennen, V. P. (2001). *The design and facilitation of asynchronous discussion activities in web-based courses: Implications for instructional design theory*. Unpublished doctoral dissertation, Indiana University, Bloomington, IN.

Dennen, V. P. (2005). From message posting to learning dialogues: Factors affecting learner participation in asynchronous discussion. *Distance Education, 26*(1), 127–148.

Dysthe, O. (2002). The learning potential of a web-mediated discussion in a university course. *Studies in Higher Education, 27*(3), 339–352.

Gao, F. (2011). Designing a discussion environment to promote connected and sustained online discussion. *Journal of Educational Multimedia and Hypermedia, 20*(1), 43–59.

Garrison, D. R., Anderson, T., & Archer, W. (2001). Critical thinking, cognitive presence, and computer conferencing in distance education. *The American Journal of Distance Education, 15*(1), 7–23.

Gilbert, P. K., & Dabbagh, N. (2005). How to structure online discussions for meaningful discourse: A case study. *British Journal of Educational Technology, 36*(1), 5–18.

Girasoli, A. J., & Hannafin, R. D. (2008). Using asynchronous AV communication tools to increase academic self-efficacy. *Computers & Education, 51*, 1676–1682.

Gunawardena, C. N., Lowe, C. A., & Anderson, T. (1997). Analysis of a global online debate and the development of an interaction analysis model for examining social construction of knowledge in computer conferencing. *Journal Educational Computing Research, 17*(4), 397–431.

Guzdial, M., & Turns, J. (2000). Effective discussion through a computer-mediated anchored forum. *Journal of the Learning Sciences, 9*(4), 437–469.

Hew, K. F., Cheung, W. S., & Jumain, S. N. (2010a). Critical thinking in asynchronous online discussions: Examining the role of the student facilitator. In Z. Abas et al. (Eds.), *Proceedings of Global Learn Asia Pacific 2010* (pp. 4210–4215). Chesapeake, VA: Association for the Advancement of Computing in Education.

Hewitt, J., & Teplovs, C. (1999). An analysis of growth patterns in computer conferencing threads. In C. Hoadley & J. Roschelle (Eds.), *Proceedings of the Computer Support for Collaborative Learning (CSCL) 1999 Conference*, Dec. 12–15. Palo Alto, CA: Stanford University.

Hummel, H. G. K., Burgos, D., Tattersall, C., Brouns, F., Kurvers, H., & Koper, R. (2005). Encouraging contributions in learning networks using incentive mechanisms. *Journal of Computer Assisted Learning, 21*, 355–365.

Jeong, A., & Frazier, S. (2008). How day of posting affects growth patterns of asynchronous discussion threads and computer-supported collaborative argumentation. *British Journal of Educational Technology, 39*(5), 875–887.

Jung, I., Choi, S., Lim, C., & Leem, J. (2002). Effects of different types of interaction on learning achievement, satisfaction and participation in web-based instruction. *Innovations in Education and Teaching International, 39*(2), 153–162.

Kear, K. (2001). Following the thread in computer conferences. *Computers & Education, 37*, 81–99.

Kear, K., & Heap, N. W. (2007). 'Sorting the wheat from the chaff': Investigating overload in educational discussion systems. *Journal of Computer Assisted Learning, 23*, 235–247.

Khan, S. (2005). Listservs in the college science classroom: Evaluating participation and ''richness'' in computer-mediated discourse. *Journal of Technology and Teacher Education, 13*(2), 325–351.

Kienle, A., & Ritterskamp, C. (2007). Facilitating asynchronous discussions in learning communities: The impact of moderation strategies. *Behaviour & Information Technology, 26*(1), 73–80.

Koh, J. H. L., Herring, S. C., & Hew, K. F. (2010). Project-based learning and student knowledge construction during asynchronous online discussion. *Internet and Higher Education, 13*, 284–291.

Lazonder, A. W., Wilhelm, P., & Ootes, A. A. W. (2003). Using sentence openers to foster student interaction in computer-mediated learning environments. *Computers & Education, 41*, 291–308.

Lu, L. L., & Jeng, I. (2006). Knowledge construction in inservice teacher online discourse: Impacts of instructor roles and facilitative strategies. *Journal of Research on Technology in Education, 39*(2), 183–202.

Marriott, P. & Hiscock, J. (2002). Voice vs Text-based Discussion Forums: an implementation of Wimba Voice Boards. In M. Driscoll & T. Reeves (Eds.), *Proceedings of World Conference on E-Learning in Corporate, Government, Healthcare, and Higher Education 2002* (pp. 640–646). Chesapeake, VA: AACE.

Masters, K., & Oberprieler, G. (2004). Encouraging equitable online participation through curriculum articulation. *Computers and Education, 42*, 319–332.

McIntosh, S., Braul, B., & Chao, T. (2003). A case study in asynchronous voice conferencing for language instruction. *Educational Media International, 40*(1), 63–74.

Nandi, D., Hamilton, M., Harland, J., & Warburton, G. (2011). How active are students in online discussion forums. In J. Hamer & M. de Raadt. (Eds.), *Proceedings of the 13th Australasian Computing Education Conference 2011* (Vol. 114, pp. 125–134). Perth, Australia: Australia Computer Society.

Newman, D. R., Webb, B., & Cochrane, C. (1995). A content analysis method to measure critical thinking in face-to-face and computer supported group learning. *Interpersonal Computing and Technology, 3*(2), 56–77.

Ng, C. S. L., Cheung, W. S., & Hew, K. F. (2010). Solving ill-structured problems in asynchronous online discussions: Built-in scaffolds vs no scaffolds. *Interactive Learning Environments, 18*(2), 115–134.

Nussbaum, E. M., Hartley, K., Sinatra, G. M., Reynolds, R. E., & Bendixen, L. D. (2002). *Enhancing the quality of online discussions*. Paper presented at the annual meeting of the American Educational Research Association, New Orleans, LA.

Oliver, M., & Shaw, G. P. (2003). Asynchronous discussion in support of medical education. *Journal of Asynchronous Learning Networks, 7*(1), 56–67.

Painter, C., Coffin, C., & Hewings, A. (2003). Impacts of directed tutorial activities in computer conferencing: A case study. *Distance Education, 24*(2), 159–174.

Poscente, K. R., & Fahy, P. J. (2003). Investigating triggers in CMC text transcripts. *The International Review of Research in Open and Distance Learning, 4*(2). Retrieved on June 26, 2007 from http://www.irrodl.org/index.php/irrodl/article/view/141/221.

Ross, S. M., & Morrison, G. R. (1997). *Getting started in instructional technology research* (3rd ed.). Bloomington, IN: Association for Educational Communications and Technology.

Salam, S., & Hew, K. F. (2010). Enhancing social studies students' critical thinking through blogcast and socratic questioning: A Singapore case study. *International Journal of Instructional Media, 37*(4), 391–401.

Schellens, T., Keer, H. V., De Wever, B., & Valcke, M. (2009). Tagging thinking types in asynchronous discussion groups: effects on critical thinking. *Interactive Learning Environments, 17*(1), 77–94.

Schellens, T., Keer, H. V., & Valcke, M. (2005). The impact of role assignment on knowledge construction in asynchronous discussion groups. *Small Group Research, 36*(6), 704–745.

Skinner, E. (2009). Using community development theory to improve student engagement in online discussion: a case study. *ALT-J, Research in Learning Technology, 17*(2), 89–100.

Strang, K. D. (2011). How can discussion forum questions be effective in online MBA courses? *Campus-Wide Information Systems, 28*(2), 80–92.

Tagg, A. C., & Dickinson, J. A. (1995). Tutor messaging and its effectiveness in encouraging student participation on computer conferences. *Journal of Distance Education, 10*(2). Retrieved on November 29, 2006 from http://cade.athabascau.ca/vol10.2/taggdickinson.html.

Thomas, M. J. W. (2002). Learning within incoherent structures: the space of online discussion forums. *Journal of Computer Assisted Learning, 18*, 351–366.

Wasko, M. M., & Faraj, S. (2000). "It is what one does:" Why people participate and help others in electronic communities of practice. *Journal of Strategic Information Systems, 9*, 155–173.

Xie, K., DeBacker, T. K., & Ferguson, C. (2006). Extending the traditional classroom through online discussion: The role of student motivation. *Journal of Educational Computing Research, 34*(1), 67–89.

Yaneske, E., & Oates, B. (2010). Using Voice Boards: pedagogical design, technological implementation, evaluation and reflections. *ALT-J Research in Learning Technology, 18*(3), 233–250.

Yang, Y.-T. C. (2008). A catalyst for teaching critical thinking in a large university class in Taiwan: Asynchronous online discussions with the facilitation of teaching assistants. *Educational Technology Research and Development, 56*, 241–264.

Yang, Y.-T. C., Newby, T. J., & Bill, R. L. (2005). Using Socratic questioning to promote critical thinking skills through asynchronous discussion forums in distance learning environments. *American Journal of Distance Education, 19*(3), 163–181.

Yang, Y.-T. C., Newby, T., & Bill, R. (2008). Facilitating interactions through structured web-based bulletin boards: A quasi-experimental study on promoting learners' critical thinking skills. *Computers & Education, 50*(4), 1572–1585.

Yeh, H. T., & Buskirk, E. V. (2005). An instructor's methods of facilitating students' participation in asynchronous online discussion. In C. Crawford, D. A. Willis, R. Carlsen, I. Gibson, K. McFerrin, J. Price, and R. Weber (Eds.), *Proceedings of Society for Information Technology and Teacher Education International Conference* 2005 (pp. 682-688). Chesapeake, VA: AACE.

Yeh, H.-T., & Lahman, M. (2007). Pre-service teachers' perceptions of asynchronous online discussion on Blackboard. *The Qualitative Report, 12*(4), 680–704.

Chapter 4
Discussion on Strategy Dilemmas

In this section, we discuss five main strategy dilemmas that educators might encounter: (a) use of grades or marks, (b) use of number of posting guideline and posting deadlines, (c) use of message labels or sentence openers (online scaffolds), (d) extending the duration of the online discussion, and (e) instructor-facilitation. As mentioned earlier, strategy dilemmas are strategies that previous empirical research had shown mixed results for, upon their implementation. Acknowledging these dilemmas is essential for educators and researchers to make informed decisions about the discussion strategies they are considering/implementing in future.

4.1 Use of Grades or Marks

Bullen (1998) found that the grades or marks associated with participation did not necessarily result in more participation for some students. These students used the marks as part of a type of cost-benefit analysis to determine how to apportion their time. Students responded to the marks, but not necessarily with enthusiasm. Their contribution was not particularly original or insightful, but often a rehash of what others had said in order to get the marks.

This was echoed by Oliver and Shaw (2003) who found that students were merely "playing the game" of assessment (p. 64). Students simply made postings to earn marks, but rarely contributed otherwise. Yeh and Buskirk (2005) similarly found that although grading the discussion was found to be the best intervention to enhance student posting, the majority of students did not further interact with their peers. In other words, students were not so much interested in exchanging ideas with their course mates as telling the instructor that they had posted their messages, so that they would not get a bad grade.

This was confirmed by Palmer et al. (2008), who reported that the frequency of postings was generally kept to the required minimum that allowed students to be

K. F. Hew and W. S. Cheung, *Student Participation in Online Discussions*,
DOI: 10.1007/978-1-4614-2370-6_4,

awarded the assignment mark. Students tended to merely fulfill the minimum (e.g. one new post and one reply per week) to qualify for the assignment marks offered (i.e. 10 % of the course marks). Cheung and Hew (2005) found that while the awarding of marks served the purpose of encouraging students to contribute in the discussion, some students felt pressurized to make themselves heard. As a result, their messages ended up sounding very similar to one another. Brewer and Klein (2006) found that groups of students who were given specific incentives or rewards (e.g. bonus points for the week's assignment) had more off-task behaviors (i.e. making statements about topics not related to the course), as compared to those who did not have incentives or rewards.

Due to this dilemma, the mere awarding of marks to increase student contribution may not be the best strategy. In view of this, several researchers (Baron and Keller 2003; Jackson 2010; McNamara and Burton 2010) have proposed the use of a set of rubrics that clearly states the allocation of marks for the different categories of contribution. Constructed rubrics that describe the specific desired outcomes of contributions to online discussions ought to, on face value, address students' expectations and steer their contributions in deeper, more meaningful directions (Jackson 2010). Studies such as that of Bai (2009) assure us that the use of rubrics is worthwhile. However, more evidence is still needed to show that the use of rubrics indeed has a direct relationship with higher frequency and quality of participation (Jackson 2010).

An alternative option is to ask students to peer evaluate one another's contributions in the online discussions. For example, at the end of each discussion assignment, individual students could fill out a peer evaluation form to identify those who have been active, whose contribution have been useful (and explain why), as well as those who did not participate or who had merely played the game of assessment. In order for the peer evaluation process to work fairly, Lewis (2006) suggested the use of anonymity. For tracking and accountability purposes, the evaluator's name is required on the form but the results can only be seen by the instructor, not by other students. In addition, Lewis (2006) suggested that the instructor has the flexibility to change the individual student's participation marks based on his or her observations in the online discussions.

4.2 Use of Number of Posting Guideline and Posting Deadlines

Although Dennen (2005) found that students needed to know how many messages they were expected to post (i.e., number of posting guideline) so that they would be interested to contribute in the discussion, other researchers disagree about the efficacy of such an approach. Researchers (e.g., Pena-Shaff and Nicholls 2004) have found that giving specific guidelines on the number of postings per week reduced students' contribution and interaction with their peers. This is because students tended to cease contributing for the week once they achieved the required number of postings stipulated by the instructor.

Other researchers found that the *quality* of the discussion could suffer too. For example, Murphy and Coleman (2004) found the quality of the discussion declined when students were forced by the course requirement to post messages in relation to a number of posting guideline. Students, for instance, found the perfunctory posts to be extremely dull, or superficial (e.g., making very general comments and "me too" additions), unlike other forums that had no requirement on the number of messages that must be posted.

With regard to the use of posting deadlines, Bullen (1998) found that they were only partly successful and might have some unintended impacts on participation. Students felt that the discussion was limited, because some students procrastinated and only posted when the deadline was fast approaching, which then left no time for follow-up responses. Dennen (2005) found that discussion deadlines served as both a participation motivator and a discussion inhibitor. In classes that did not require consistent and ongoing dialog, discussion deadlines dictated the timing of much student participation, with clusters of messages posted within the few days leading up to a deadline. While discussion deadlines were effective at generating participation, it often stifled actual dialog conversation development because students were merely racing to post messages by the due date, as opposed to reading and responding to each other's messages. The latter activity would require contribution at multiple points in time, which, generally, was not feasible when all students were contributing at the last minute.

So, how then should deadlines be structured? As of now, no conclusive finding has been reported in the literature. Bullen (1998) suggested that deadlines should perhaps be established near the midpoint of the discussion, so that adequate time is allowed for follow-up comments. Instructors may also consider establishing two deadlines, one for the initial contribution and a second for a follow-up comment (Bullen 1998). Instructors should also perhaps encourage students to respond to one another within 24–48 h. Such a strategy might be a more viable option than simply imposing two or three major deadlines throughout the duration of the online discussion. However, we are not sure if these suggestions would work because students may still choose to wait until the last moment to post. We urge future research to examine this further.

An alternative option would be to use other forms of incentives, such as a rewards program that combines quantitative and qualitative measures to motivate student contribution, instead of using mere quantitative measures. Such a reward program is similar to the frequent flyer program that airline companies have adopted. For example, in Hummel et al.'s (2005a) study, the reward mechanism allowed individual students to gain personal access to additional course-related information that are useful and relevant to their studies through the accumulation of points earned by making postings to discussion forums. This additional course information was not available elsewhere.

The reward system, which included both quantitative and qualitative components, awarded participants with points for activities such as making contributions in the discussion (20 points for each post), replying to posts (10 points each), and rating a posts (3 points for each). On the qualitative side, contributors received points: each time their contributions prompted a reply (5 points for each reply to a post), and each time their posting was rated by their peers (3 points × rating value), where ratings ranged from 1 (very poor) to 5 (very good) (Hummel et al. 2005a). The qualitative measure was included to encourage participants to provide contributions that would benefit the online discussion. A threshold of 33 points, with just one post, one reply, and one rating, was needed to gain access to the extra course-related materials. Results showed that the level of contribution indeed increased with the introduction of the incentive system. Interestingly, participants continued contributing even after the reward was withdrawn.

Also, delineating certain expectations of what the postings should entail, such as requiring students to provide reasons or explanations for their "I agree" statements, might be a better alternative, as compared to merely providing a set of guidelines for the number of required postings.

4.3 Use of Sentence Openers or Message Labels

Not all scholars agree that the use of sentence openers or message labels could positively impact student contribution in online discussions. Typically, the types of online messages that participants could post are constrained to a predefined set of sentence openers or message labels embedded within the discussion forum. This could lead to some unexpected consequences. The use of these sentence openers or message labels could cause disruption to the online discussion, as they force participants to interact in an unnatural way (Beers et al. 2005; Dillenbourg 2002). Participants, for example, could not raise a point at the moment they wished to raise it, because a prior contribution must be closed before a new one can be made (Beers et al. 2005). This could disrupt students' thoughts, and subsequently stunt the flow of the discussion.

Jeong and Joung (2007) examined the impact of message labels on collaborative argumentation in asynchronous online discussions. In one group, students posted messages using a prescribed set of message categories such as argument, evidence, critique, and explanation. Another group was told to explicitly label their online messages with these message categories. A control group used none of the categories and labels. The researchers found that the message labels inhibited the thinking processes needed to produce critical argumentation in an online discussion. Results suggested that students who use message labels are two to three times less likely to critique postings by other students, and two to three times less likely to respond back to their peers' critiques to defend their own previous claims. The label used to identify critiques might have discouraged students from posting critiques. For example, the label "CRIT" carried negative connotations which could have made students perceive posting critiques as being overly confrontational. Perhaps a less confrontational label could be considered for future use, so as to encourage participants to critique one another's postings.

In another study, Ng et al. (2010) found no significant difference among students who had access to sentence openers and message labels and those who did not, in terms of the mean number of message posted. The researchers found that as much as 52.6 % of the online posts were wrongly labeled. In other words, participants may use the message labels in a way that is not necessarily consistent with the meaning provided by the designers (Baker et al. 1999). Further analysis of the Ng et al. (2010) study suggested that the participants were not clear about the distinction among message labels, in particular the "Identify problems," and the "Discuss problems" labels. One possible solution to this problem would be to explain each message label clearly to the participants, and provide them with examples of message postings that fall under each message label category. In addition, if students were reluctant to openly disagree with others, they need to be encouraged to do so. Perhaps, one viable way to invite argumentation would be to include sentence openers and incorporating the Socratic questioning approach (Ng et al. 2010). Socratic questioning can probe students to exchange viewpoints, explore various solutions to problems, as well as consider the implications of solutions (Ng et al. 2010). However, this suggestion is still currently based merely on conjectures. Future research should be conducted to verify this claim.

Overall, we found that the findings related to the use of sentence openers or message labels are not conclusive at this stage, and so there is a necessity for future research. Dillenbourg (2002) argued that the challenge is not to formulate a golden script, but rather to understand why some scripts are effective and others are not. In other words, it would be useful if future studies could examine the specific conditions under which scripts are most effective, as well as the conditions in which they do not function. This would enable scholars to chart a possible road map or guideline for educators to use.

4.4 Extending the Duration of the Online Discussion

Some scholars attribute the issue of lack of time to the following reason: there is insufficient time for discussion in an online setting, because involvement in online discussions typically takes more time than it does in a traditional, face-to-face class. Due to this claim, the suggestion to extend the duration of online discussions has been made in order to allow students to have more time to think and contribute to the discussion (e.g., Jeong and Frazier 2008; Yeh and Lahman 2007).

However, in a series of studies that we conducted (Hew and Cheung 2009, 2010a, b, 2011a) we found no evidence for such a claim or suggestion. For example, we found no supporting evidence for the hypothesis that discussion forums that had more messages posted enjoyed longer length of online discussion than the forums where users posted less frequently in (Hew and Cheung 2009, 2010a). Neither was there a correlation between the duration of the discussion and the frequency of higher level knowledge constructions (Hew and Cheung 2010b, 2011a).

Moreover, Brown and Green (2009) found that the average student spent about 1 h per week reading the messages posted in an online discussion. Based on the assumption that it takes less than 2 h to compose initial messages and responses to the discussion prompt, the time commitment required for an online discussion was found to be similar to that of traditional, face-to-face courses. Overall, the results of the study suggested that asynchronous discussion activities used in online learning is comparable to face-to-face classes in terms of the time needed for weekly participation.

Therefore, we suggest that the issue at hand may actually be a matter of priority choices or personal preference, rather than a lack of time per se. How students prioritize a particular activity over another will determine how much time they are willing to spend on it. So, the problem of not having enough time for the discussion may not be a problem in itself, but rather, it is indicative of a failure to prioritize. For example, many students in Gerbic's (2006) study tended to view work and family commitments as more urgent or more important as compared to contributing in online discussions, hence the discussions were placed on a lower prioritizing, and were subsequently overlooked. Similarly, many participants in Hammond's (1999) study felt that they had too many demands made on them at work and at home, and that allocating time to participate in online discussions meant restructuring their priorities, and some people were reluctant to do so.

The problem of a lack of priorities may be compounded by the fact that students do not see one another face-to-face in online discussions, as well as the time-independent nature of the forums. This is perhaps best captured by the adage: *Out of sight, out of mind.* Students feel less pressurized to participate in the online discussions, as they could delay participation, or even get out of the habit of participating altogether (Hammond 1999). In contrast, there is peer pressure to take part in face-to-face discussions simply because everyone is physically present, and the activities are clearly timetabled (Hammond 1999).

Probably, the only way to manage the prioritizing problem is to create a sense of great need or urgency for the online discussions. If students are able to view the online discussions as being important, they will be able to adjust their schedules in such a way that they can find time to contribute in the discussions. On the other hand, if the discussions are not seen as being important, students will have the tendency to procrastinate. Students need to see the value for participating in online discussions. Perhaps, using the online discussions to complement the course or add value to it in a way that surpasses other ways (e.g., the strategies that we described earlier from the findings of Hummel et al. 2005a, b and Guzdial and Turns 2000) would be helpful.

4.5 Use of Instructor Facilitation

The instructor, traditionally, takes on the role of an online facilitator. The responsibilities of a facilitator may be classified into three different types: organizational, social, intellectual, and technical (Berge 1995; Paulsen 1995).

Table 4.1 Description of activity related to the organizational, social and intellectual facilitation types

Facilitation type	Description of activity	Source
Organizational	Spur participation when it is lagging. For example, request direct comments and responses to the issues discussed	Paulsen (1995)
	Require regular participation. For example, exhorting students to post at least two messages per week	Klemm (1998), Paulsen (1995)
	Prompt frequently. Use private messages to urge participants to take part in the discussion, to initiate debates, and to solicit suggestions	Paulsen (1995)
	Encourage participants to respond to each other as well as to the tutor	Salter (2000)
	Keep discussion on track	Winiecki and Chyung (1998)
Social	Be responsive. For example, respond quickly to every contribution either by posting a personal message to the contributor or by referring to the author's comment in the discussion	Paulsen (1995)
	Reinforce good discussant behaviors. For example, praise students who respond effectively online	Berge (1995)
	Encourage students to introduce themselves to help build a sense of community	Berge (1995)
Intellectual	Ask questions to help participants understand	O'Grady (2001)
	Challenge ideas or opinions. Draw attention to opposing perspectives, different directions, or conflicting opinions	Paulsen (1995); Goodyear et al. (2001); Berge (1995)
Intellectual	Insist that opinions posted by participants are supported with data and rational reasoning	Klemm (1998)
Technical	Help students be familiar with the online discussion environment	Berge (1995), Salmon (2004)

Adapted from Cheung and Hew (2005), pp. 58–59

Based on Paulsen's framework (1995) as well as other researchers' work (e.g., Berge 1995; Cheung and Hew 2005; Goodyear et al. 2001; Klemm 1998; O'Grady 2001; Salmon 2004; Salter 2000; Winiecki and Chyung 1998), the role of facilitation may be summarized into Table 4.1.

Some researchers recommend that an instructor monitors the discussion for the reasons of keeping the discussion on track, engaging the students, helping participants overcome technical problems, establishing the rules, and setting common expectations for the discussion (e.g. no personal attacks), among others (Beaudin 1999; Cifuentes et al. 1997; Lang 2000; Yeh and Lahman 2007). It is important to note that, although instructors play an important role in facilitating online asynchronous discussions, not all researchers agree that an instructor/facilitator is the best choice.

Firstly, facilitating an online discussion could be time consuming. Hiltz (1988) described it as being a parent: "You are on duty all the time, and there seems to be no end to the demands on your time and energy" (p. 441). Having the instructor take on the role of facilitator may not be the best choice, because not all instructors are able to dedicate the amount of time and energy needed to facilitate the discussions (Correia and Baran 2010; Seo 2007).

Secondly, findings from previous research suggested that instructor/facilitation may result in instructor-centered discussion (Light et al. 2000), and inhibit students' participation and voice (Pearson 1999; Zhao and McDougall 2005). Students, typically, see the instructor as an expert, and so the instructor's postings may deter students from contributing their thoughts and comments, because students consider the instructor's comment as the final, authoritative one (Zhao and McDougall 2005). Dysthe (2002) differentiated between asymmetrical and symmetrical discussions. In asymmetrical discussions, communication lines tend to center upon the instructor, whose authority rests on status, power, and knowledge; while in symmetrical discussions, communication lines tend to focus on the students (Dsythe 2002). Dysthe argued that by staying out of a discussion, the instructor could stimulate symmetrical discussions among the students and give each student voice more authority.

An et al. (2009) found that when the instructor's facilitation was kept to a minimum, students tended to express their thoughts and opinions more freely. Arend (2009) reported that in forums that exhibited lower level critical thinking, the instructors were very active in the online discussions, sometimes responding to nearly every student post. Correia and Baran (2010) found that many students treated the discussion questions as short answer essay questions instead of interactive discussions when the discussion was facilitated by the instructor. Dennen (2005) found that when the instructor was involved in the online discussion, students responded to the instructor's comments instead of one another's. As Rourke and Anderson (2002, p. 4) warned, "Ultimately, the concern is that instructor-led discussions can easily revert to the recitation structure, or initiate-respond-evaluate structure, of a traditional lecture."

Furthermore, in a large study that examined over 40,000 postings from a total of 375 discussion forums, Mazzolini and Maddison (2007) found that the percentage of discussion threads started by instructors showed significant negative correlations with both the length of discussion threads and the student posting rate. Results also showed that the percentage of instructor postings within a forum yielded a significant negative correlation with the length of discussion threads, as well as a significant negative correlation with the student posting rate. In summary, Mazzolini and Maddison (2007) concluded that the more the instructors posted, the less frequently students posted, and the shorter were the discussion threads.

4.6 The Case for Peer Facilitation

One possible strategy to circumvent these concerns is to have students facilitate the online discussions. There exists two variants of student facilitation. The first variant is called same-age (after Smet et al. 2008) or peer facilitation which refers to students from the same course facilitating the online discussion. The second variant is called cross-age (after Smet et al. 2008) facilitation, which refers to older students facilitating the discussion of younger students, such as graduate students or research assistants facilitating undergraduate students' online discussions (e.g., Murphy et al. 1996). Although in both cases the instructor is not involved in the online discussion, we felt that the cross-age student facilitation is akin to instructor facilitation. After all, younger students tend to rely on older students for guidance and input. It is, therefore, not unreasonable to assume that younger students perceive the graduate students as instructors who provide explanations for issues or questions asked or suggestions for problems discussed.

There is less research done on same-age or peer facilitation, than instructor, or cross-age facilitation (Baran and Correia 2009; Hew and Cheung 2008; Hew et al. 2010b; Ikpeze 2007). Results of previous research on peer facilitation suggested that students felt more comfortable vocalizing their views, brainstorming for ideas, and challenging one another's ideas in a peer-facilitated discussion environment (e.g., Correia and Davis 2007; Hew et al. 2010a, b; Rourke and Anderson 2002). For example, Rourke and Anderson (2002) reported that a majority of students expressed a preference for peer-facilitated discussions over instructor-facilitated ones, explaining that peer-facilitated discussions invited more response (i.e. more messages being posted per week). Tagg (1994) selected two students from his class to act as peer facilitators. One of them was assigned to set the agenda for the discussion and post initial contributions, while the other helped summarize the discussions. Tagg (1994) found that the involvement of the peer facilitators increased student participation rates, as well as students' understanding of the content.

Students' posts were also found to be significantly longer in length in weeks where they were in charge of facilitating the discussion (Poole 2000). A peer-facilitated online discussion forum was also found to contain significantly more posts responding to previous comments, as well as more substantive responses than those found in a nonpeer-facilitated one (Seo 2007). A message was deemed to be substantive if the student offered an appropriate interpretation, inference, or justification in explaining his or her views, while a message that did not add such an element was treated as a nonsubstantive response (Seo 2007). Baran and Correia (2009) identified three peer facilitation strategies that generated innovative ideas, motivated students to participate, and created a relaxed environment for online discussion: (1) inspirational (i.e., asking participants to imagine idealistic scenarios, search for inner goals, and discuss ways to achieve them), (2) practice oriented (i.e., encouraging participants to reflect on real-life situations and their actual teaching and learning contexts with constant connections to the readings), and (3) highly structured (i.e., organizing the discussion around the questions of what the participants already knew, wanted to know, and learned before and after reading the assigned chapter for the week).

Thanks to the aforementioned research, we have a better understanding of peer facilitation. However, despite the potential of peer facilitation in asynchronous discussions, Correia and Baran (2010) argues that more research needs to be done in order to better understand its use. Some extant, research on peer facilitation is limited because the actual types of peer facilitation techniques were not clearly explained. For example, in Gilbert and Dabbagh's (2005) study, peer facilitators were provided with facilitation guidelines that included an article entitled "The role of the online instructor/facilitator", which was a web-based resource explaining the various facilitator roles in an online discussion. What exactly these roles entailed were not elaborated.

Some fundamental questions or issues are still not fully addressed. For example, what exactly motivates participants to contribute in a peer-facilitated discussion environment? How can participants' discussion be sustained in a peer-facilitated environment? Also, how can higher or advanced levels of knowledge construction be fostered in peer-facilitated online discussions?

In Chaps. 5, 6 and 7, we report ten empirical studies conducted to examine peer facilitation and how it could promote the following three outcomes: (1) increase students' online contribution rate, (2) sustain students' online discussion, and (3) foster higher levels of knowledge construction. However, it is important to note that, peer facilitation should not be viewed as a "cure-all" or panacea for all online discussion issues or challenges. Hence, in Chap. 8, we discuss certain conditions or situations that may best be addressed using peer or instructor facilitation. We report a study in Chap. 8 that attempt to answer this issue.

References

An, H., Shin, S., & Lim, K. (2009). The effects of different instructor facilitation approaches on students' interactions during asynchronous online discussions. *Computers and Education, 53*, 749–760.

Arend, B. (2009). Encouraging critical thinking in online threaded discussions. *The Journal of Educators Online, 6*(1). Retrieved on February 15, 2012 from http://www.thejeo.com/Archives/Volume6Number1/Arendpaper.pdf.

Bai, H. (2009). Facilitating students' critical thinking in online discussion: An instructor's experience. *Journal of Interactive Online Learning, 8*(2), 156–164.

Baker, M., Hansen, T., Joiner, R., & Traum, D. (1999). The role of grounding in collaborative learning tasks. In P. Dillenbourg (Ed.), *Collaborative learning: Cognitive and computational approaches* (pp. 31–63). Oxford: Pergamon.

Baran, E., & Correia, A.-P. (2009). Student-led facilitation strategies in online discussions. *Distance Education, 30*(3), 339–361.

Baron, J., & Keller, M. (2003). Use of rubrics in online assessment. In the Evaluations and Assessment Conference 2003. Adelaide: University of South Australia.

Beaudin, B. P. (1999). Keeping online asynchronous discussions on topic. *Journal of Asynchronous Learning Networks, 3*(2), 41–53.
Beers, P. J., Boshuizen, H. P. A., Kirschner, P. A., & Gijselaers, W. H. (2005). Computer support for knowledge construction in collaborative learning environments. *Computers in Human Behavior, 21*, 623–643.
Berge, Z. L. (1995). Facilitating computer conferencing: Recommendations from the field. *Educational Technology, 35*(1), 22–30.
Brewer, S., & Klein, J. D. (2006). Types of positive interdependence and affiliation motive in an asynchronous, collaborative learning environment. *Educational Technology Research and Development, 54*(4), 331–354.
Bullen, M. (1998). Participation and critical thinking in online university distance education. *Journal of Distance Education, 13*(2). Retrieved on February 23, 2012 from http://www.jofde.ca/index.php/jde/article/view/140/394.
Cheung, W. S., & Hew, K. F. (2005). Factors affecting learners' satisfaction on the use of asynchronous online discussion in a hypermedia design environment. *Journal of Southeast Asian Education, 5*(1&2), 56–70.
Cifuentes, L., Murphy, K. L., Segur, R., & Kodali, S. (1997). Design considerations for computer conferences. *Journal of Research on Computing in Education, 30*(2), 177–201.
Correia, A. P., & Baran, E. (2010). Lessons learned on facilitating asynchronous discussions for online learning. *Educacao, Formacao & Tecnologias, 3*(1), 59–67.
Correia, A. P., & Davis, N. E. (2007). The design of collaboration in the virtual classroom. In M. Simonson (Ed.), *30th annual proceedings of selected papers on the practice of educational communications and technology* (pp. 84–87). Bloomington, IN: Association for Educational Communications and Technology.
Dennen, V. P. (2005). From message posting to learning dialogues: Factors affecting learner participation in asynchronous discussion. *Distance Education, 26*(1), 127–148.
Dillenbourg, P. (2002). Over-scripting CSCL: The risks of blending collaborative learning with instructional design. In P. A. Kirschner (Ed.), *Three worlds of CSCL: Can we support CSCL?* (pp. 61–91). Heerlen: Open Universiteit Nederland.
Dysthe, O. (2002). The learning potential of a web-mediated discussion in a university course. *Studies in Higher Education, 27*(3), 339–352.
Gerbic, P. (2006). To post or not to post: Undergraduate student perceptions about participating in online discussions. In *Who's learning? Whose technology? Proceedings Ascilite Sydney* 2006. Retrieved on January 27, 2012 from http://www.ascilite.org.au/conferences/sydney06/proceeding/pdf_papers/p124.pdf.
Goodyear, P., Salmon, G., Spector, J. M., Steeples, C., & Tickner, S. (2001). Competences for online teaching: A special report. *Educational Technology Research and Development, 49*(1), 65–72.
Guzdial, M., & Turns, J. (2000). Effective discussion through a computer-mediated anchored forum. *Journal of the Learning Sciences, 9*(4), 437–469.
Hammond, M. (1999). Issues associated with participation in on line forums—The case of the communicative learner. *Education and Information Technologies, 4*(4), 353–367.
Hew, K. F., & Cheung, W. S. (2008). Attracting student participation in asynchronous online discussions: A case study of peer facilitation. *Computers & Education, 51*, 1111–1124.
Hew, K. F., & Cheung, W. S. (2009). Participation in student-facilitated discussion forums: An empirical analysis of facilitators' habits of mind. In B. H. Tan & S. R. Galea (Eds.), *Proceedings of the 14th International Conference on Thinking 2009* (pp. 268–279). Kuala Lumpur: Universiti Putra Malaysia.
Hew, K. F., & Cheung, W. S. (2010a). Possible factors influencing Asian students' degree of participation in peer-facilitated online discussion forums: A case study. *Asia Pacific Journal of Education, 30*(1), 85–104.
Hew, K. F., & Cheung, W. S. (2010b). Fostering higher knowledge construction levels in online discussion forums: An exploratory case study. *International Journal of Web-based Learning and Teaching Technologies, 5*(4), 44–55.

Hew, K. F., & Cheung, W. S. (2011). Higher-level knowledge construction in asynchronous online discussions: An analysis of group size, duration of online discussion, and student facilitation techniques. *Instructional Science, 39*(3), 303–319.

Hew, K. F., Cheung, W. S., & Jumain, S. N. (2010a). Critical thinking in asynchronous online discussions: Examining the role of the student facilitator. In Z. Abas, et al. (Eds.), *Proceedings of global learn Asia Pacific 2010* (pp. 4210–4215). Chesapeake, VA: Association for the Advancement of Computing in Education.

Hew, K. F., Cheung, W. S., & Ng, C. S. L. (2010b). Student contribution in asynchronous online discussion: a review of the research and empirical exploration. *Instructional Science, 38*(6), 571–606.

Hiltz. R. S. (1988). *Learning in a virtual classroom. Final evaluation report* (Vol. 25). Newark, N.J.: Computerized Conferencing and Communications Centre.

Hummel, H. G. K., Burgos, D., Tattersall, C., Brouns, F., Kurvers, H., & Koper, R. (2005a). Encouraging contributions in learning networks using incentive mechanisms. *Journal of Computer Assisted Learning, 21*, 355–365.

Hummel, H. G. K., Tattersall, C., Burgos, D., Brouns, F., Kurvers, H., & Koper, R. (2005b). Facilitating participation: From the EML web site to the learning network for learning design. *Interactive Learning Environments, 13*(1–2), 55–69.

Ikpeze, C. (2007). Small group collaboration in peer-led electronic discourse: An analysis of group dynamics and interactions involving preservice and inservice teachers. *Journal of Technology and Teacher Education, 15*(3), 383–407.

Jackson, K. (2010). What value assessment rubrics in shaping students' engagement in asynchronous online discussions? In C. H. Steel, M. J. Keppel, P. Gerbic & S. Housego (Eds.), *Curriculum, technology & transformation for an unknown future. Proceedings ascilite Sydney 2010* (pp. 454–458). Retrieved on January 27, 2012 from http://ascilite.org.au/conferences/sydney10/procs/crisp-symposium.pdf.

Jeong, A., & Frazier, S. (2008). How day of posting affects growth patterns of asynchronous discussion threads and computer-supported collaborative argumentation. *British Journal of Educational Technology, 39*(5), 875–887.

Jeong, A., & Joung, S. (2007). Scaffolding collaborative argumentation in asynchronous discussions with message constraints and message labels. *Computers & Education, 48*, 427–445.

Klemm, W. R. (1998). Eight ways to get students more engaged in online conferences. *T.H.E. Journal, 26*(1), 62–64.

Lang, D. (2000). Critical thinking in web courses. *Syllabus, 9*, 20–24.

Lewis, K. O. (2006). Evaluation of online group activities: Intra-group member peer evaluation. *Paper presented at the 22nd Annual Conference on Distance Teaching and Learning*. Retrieved on February 16, 2012 from http://www.uwex.edu/disted/conference/Resource_library/proceedings/06_4136.pdf.

Light, P., Nesbitt, E., Light, V., & White, S. (2000). Variety is the spice of life: Student use of CMC in the context of campus-based study. *Computers and Education, 34*(3), 257–267.

Mazzolini, M., & Maddison, S. (2007). When to jump in: The role of the instructor in online discussion forums. *Computers & Education, 49*, 193–213.

McNamara, J., & Burton, K. (2010). Assessment of online discussion forums for law students. *Journal of University Teaching and Learning*, *6*(2). Retrieved on August 12, 2011 from http://ro.uow.edu.au/jutlp/vol6/iss2/6.

Murphy, E., & Coleman, E. (2004). Graduate students' experiences of challenges in online asynchronous discussions. *Canadian Journal of Learning and Technology*, *30*(2). Retrieved on August 5, 2011 from http://www.cjlt.ca/index.php/cjlt/article/view/128/122.

Murphy, K. L., Cifuentes, L., Yakimovicz, A., Segur, R., Mahoney, S., & Kodali, S. (1996). Students assume the mantle of moderating computer conferences: A case study. *American Journal of Distance Education, 10*(3), 20–35.

Ng, C. S. L., Cheung, W. S., & Hew, K. F. (2010). Solving ill-structured problems in asynchronous online discussions: Built-in scaffolds vs no scaffolds. *Interactive Learning Environments, 18*(2), 115–134.

O' Grady, G. K. (2001). Maximising the potential of computer mediated discussion: guidelines for facilitation. *Centre for Development of Teaching and Learning (CDTL) Brief, 4*(4). Retrieved on September 1, 2011 from http://www.cdtl.nus.sg/Brief/v4n4/sec3.asp.

Oliver, M., & Shaw, G. P. (2003). Asynchronous discussion in support of medical education. *Journal of Asynchronous Learning Networks, 7*(1), 56–67.

Palmer, S., Holt, D., & Bray, S. (2008). Does the discussion help? The impact of a formally assessed online discussion on final student results. *British Journal of Educational Technology, 39*(5), 847–858. doi:10.1111/j.1467-8535.2007.00780.x.

Paulsen, M. F. (1995). Moderating educational computer conferences. In Z. L. Berge & M. P. Collins (Eds.), *Computer mediated communication and the online classroom: Vol. 3. Distance Learning* (pp. 81–89). Cresskill, NJ: Hampton Press, Inc.

Pearson, J. (1999). Electronic networking in initial teacher education: Is a virtual faculty of education possible? *Computers and Education, 32*(3), 221–238.

Pena-Shaff, J. B., & Nicholls, C. (2004). Analyzing student interactions and meaning construction in computer bulletin board discussions. *Computers & Education, 42*(3), 243–265.

Rourke, L., & Anderson, T. (2002). Using peer teams to lead online discussions. *Journal of Interactive Media in Education, 1*. Retrieved on August 31, 2011 from http://jime.open.ac.uk/article/2002-1/80.

Salmon, G. (2004). E-moderating: The key to teaching and learning online. London: Taylor & Francis Group.

Salter, G. (2000). Making use of online discussion groups. *Australian Educational Computing, 15*(2), 5–10.

Seo, K. K. (2007). Utilizing peer moderating in online discussions: Addressing the controversy between teacher moderation and nonmoderation. *The American Journal of Distance Education, 21*(1), 21–36.

Smet, M. D., Keer, H. V., & Valcke, M. (2008). Blending asynchronous discussion groups and peer tutoring in higher education: An exploratory study of online peer tutoring behavior. *Computers & Education, 50*, 207–223.

Tagg, A. C. (1994). Leadership from within: Student moderation of computer conferences. *American Journal of Distance Education, 8*(3), 40–50.

Winiecki, D. J., & Chyung, Y. (August, 1998). Keeping the thread: Helping distance education students and instructors keep track of asynchronous discussions. In *Proceedings of the 14th Annual Conference on Distance Teaching & Learning, 98* (pp. 451–460). Madison, WI: University of Wisconsin-Madison.

Yeh, H. T., & Buskirk, E. V. (2005). An instructor's methods of facilitating students' participation in asynchronous online discussion. In C. Crawford, D. A. Willis, R. Carlsen, I. Gibson, K. McFerrin, J. Price, & R. Weber (Eds.), *Proceedings of society for information technology and teacher education international conference 2005* (pp. 682–688). Chesapeake, VA: AACE.

Yeh, H.-T., & Lahman, M. (2007). Pre-service teachers' perceptions of asynchronous online discussion on Blackboard. *The Qualitative Report, 12*(4), 680–704.

Zhao, N., & McDougall, D. (2005). Cultural factors affecting Chinese students' participation in asynchronous online learning. In G. Richards (Ed.), *Proceedings of world conference on E-learning in corporate, government, healthcare, and higher education 2005* (pp. 2723–2729). Chesapeake, VA: AACE.

Chapter 5
Case Studies on Peer Facilitation: What Motivates Participants to Contribute?

In this chapter, we describe four studies that examined the possible factors which could motivate participants to contribute in peer facilitated online discussions. The first study examined peer facilitators' habits of mind, while the other three studies examined factors other than habits of mind that could motivate participants to contribute in online discussions. We first summarize the key elements of the studies before presenting the findings. Although we acknowledge that our studies cannot guarantee sampling representativeness, the findings from the four studies presented here nonetheless provide important information that can be applied in similar contexts and situations. We believe that these findings would be useful to other educators and researchers who are interested in using peer facilitation in their asynchronous online discussion environments. Figure 5.1 summarizes the findings.

5.1 Examining Habits of Mind

Study 1

Study 1 was conducted to address the question—What specific habits of mind exhibited by peer facilitators may influence the quantity of online messages posted by participants (Hew and Cheung 2009)? The following four habits of mind were studied: awareness of own thinking, open-mindedness, taking a position, and sensitivity to others.

Definition

Habits of mind may be viewed as the affective aspects of thinking (Neo and Cheung 2007), that is the natural disposition to employ one's skills or knowledge in deciding what to do in any circumstance. Although different authors have suggested different lists of these habits, and alternatively labeling them habits of mind (Costa and Kallick 2000; Marzano et al. 1993), habits of thought (Dewey 1933), or thinking dispositions (Ennis 1987; Facione et al. 1995), the various lists

K. F. Hew and W. S. Cheung, *Student Participation in Online Discussions*,
DOI: 10.1007/978-1-4614-2370-6_5, © Springer Science+Business Media, New York 2012

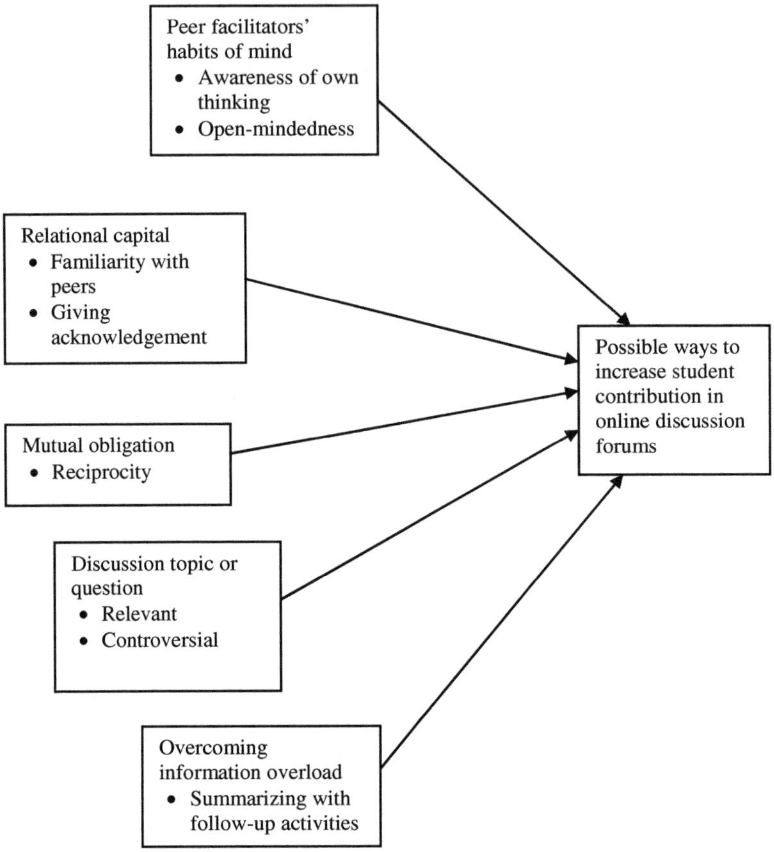

Fig. 5.1 Major findings

are quite similar in spirit (Tishman 2000). In this study, we examined four habits of mind.

Awareness of own thinking refers to the ability to know what one knows and what one does not know (Costa 2000). It is similar to metacognition. Students who display this habit of mind typically describe their thoughts when handling a task or question (Marzano et al. 1993). *Open-mindedness* refers to the habit of seeking out, as well as considering different viewpoints (Marzano et al. 1993). Students who have developed a sense of open-mindedness typically use words or phrases such as "I look forward to hearing from you…", "Let me know what you think…" *Taking a position* refers to the habit of taking a stand pertinent to an issue being discussed (Marzano et al. 1993), as well as providing justification for it. This justification may be grounded on literature-based evidence, or personal experiences. *Sensitivity to others* refers to the ability to empathize with another person's

Table 5.1 Rubric to examine habits of mind (adapted from Marzano et al. 1993)

Habits of Mind	Indicators
Is aware of own thinking	Describes the thoughts he or she uses when faced with a task, problem, or question. Describes how an awareness of own thinking helps me to improve the task
Is open-minded	Considers alternative views Seeks out different viewpoints.
Takes a position	Takes a position that is related to the circumstances Provides justification for the position
Is sensitive to others	Shows concern about others' feelings. Shows concern about others' level of knowledge Encourages respect for individual differences

feelings, show concerns about others' level of knowledge, or encourage respect for individual differences (Marzano et al. 1993).

Method

This study involved 20 discussion forums selected from two graduate courses: Course I with 13 forums, and Course II with 7 forums. There were a total of 27 students. Although the 20 forums came from two courses, they shared the following characteristics. First, both courses discussed the use of technology in education, involving a blended approach of face-to-face tutorials and asynchronous online discussion activities. Second, each forum was entirely peer facilitated. Third, all 20 forums used the same threaded asynchronous discussion tool. Fourth, students were free to contribute in whichever discussion forum they wished with no number of posting quota imposed. Fifth, all forums had the same discussion activity, which was to design instructional materials for use in schools or training organizations. Students used the discussion forums to identify design problems of their peers' design projects, give viewpoints or suggestions for improvements, and respond to the comments raised.

Since the mean number of all participant postings was 19.55 for all 20 forums, forums with 20 or more posting were deemed as the frequent forums. Seven such forums were found. Seven least frequent forums in terms of participant posting were then chosen from the remaining forums and referred to as the infrequent forums.

Data were collected through online observations of the discussion forums and a series of interviews. The online posts by peer facilitators were observed in order to examine the types of habits of mind displayed using the rubric shown in Table 5.1. Overall, inter-rater agreement of the coding was 90 %. Ten individuals volunteered to be interviewed which lasted 30 min each to gain insight into why students contributed in the online discussions.

Main Findings of Study 1

5.1.1 Peer Facilitators Should Display the Following Two Habits of Mind More Frequently: Awareness of Own Thinking and Open-Mindedness

Results from Study 1 showed that the more and less frequent forums differed significantly in terms of the frequency of the following habits of mind displayed by the peer facilitators: (a) awareness of own thinking and (b) open-mindedness. In other words, this finding suggests that participants tend to post significantly more postings in forums that are facilitated by peers who are aware of their own thinking, and who are open-minded. Why is this so?

The interview data revealed that peer facilitators who are aware of their own thinking tend to describe clearly the thoughts they use when faced with a task, problem, or question. This allows other participants to have a better understanding of what the discussion is about and hence enables them to respond to the topic being discussed. For example, Daniel (pseudonym), a participant, remarked:

> A facilitator who is aware of his own thinking tends to be clear in his postings (e.g., asking questions). This helps the other participants to understand clearly the issue being discussed. Consequently, I know what suggestions or feedback to give. If he is not clear about what he is asking or commenting, I am not sure how to respond to his message, or how to help him. As a result, I would participate less.

Discussions that are facilitated by peer facilitators who are open-minded are seen as a safe environment where participants feel they can freely post their comments without running the risk of being harshly judged or criticized. As Georgia, a participant, stated:

> Open-mindedness will definitely have an impact on my degree of contribution in a discussion. An open-minded facilitator shows that he or she is willing to consider other people's viewpoints and ideas, and welcomes suggestions and comments. This makes me more likely to contribute my opinions in the discussions.

Researchers posit that habits of mind can be cultivated through the specially crafted learning experiences that encourage and reinforce their use (Tishman et al. 1995). We propose two suggestions here. First, instructors should *model* the required habits of mind (Tishman et al. 1995). For example, to develop the habit of open-mindedness, Costa and Kallick (2000) suggested that instructors give students problems or issues that require a change of perspective to find a solution, model the habit of open-mindedness, thereafter ask students to describe how they could look at the issue differently, and what other possibilities would arise from a change in viewpoint. Instructors may also observe students' interactions, and label the habit of open-mindedness when it they occurs. For example, when a student considers her peer's suggestions, the instructor may highlight it, and compliment the student for showing the habit of open-mindedness (Neo and Cheung 2007).

Second, besides modeling, instructors should *explain* what habits of mind are, how they benefit students, and when they come into play (Tishman et al. 1995). Instructors, for example, could explain that articulating about their thinking or reasoning process (i.e., awareness of own thinking) is of great value not only in the classroom but in the world as well. Individuals who are aware of their own thinking are more able to critically analyze their own postings because they are cognizant of their own understandings and misconceptions. This facilitates the negotiation of ideas, as individuals can identify the inconsistencies and weaknesses in their own viewpoints more readily, as compared to their peers who are less cognizant of their own thinking (Hew and Cheung 2011b). Individuals who are less aware of their own reasoning processes tend to be more defensive when others point out the flaws in their viewpoints, and this renders the task of negotiating and coming to a consensus even more difficult (Hew and Cheung 2011b).

5.2 Examining Other Possible Reasons Why Students Contribute in Online Discussions

In this section, we describe three studies (Study 2, 3, and 4) that examined possible factors other than peer facilitators' habits of mind that could motivate participants to contribute in online discussions. Table 5.2 provides a summary of these three studies. Each of the three studies will be described first, followed by a cross-case discussion of the main findings.

Study 2: Full-Time Diploma in Education Students

Study 2 was carried out to investigate possible reasons that motivate full-time diploma students to contribute in online discussions (Cheung et al. 2008). The following research question was examined: Given the same nature of the discussion tasks, and that the students are given a freedom of choice to choose, why do they choose to contribute in some forums but not in others?

Method

Sixteen students, who were enrolled in a diploma in education program, participated in the study. The program was a blended course that involved both face-to-face and asynchronous online discussion sections. The online discussion activity, course expectations, time requirements, and deliverables, were similar for all students. Each student designed a Web-based learning resource and then uploaded their design onto their own discussion forum. The students facilitated their own discussion forums to discuss ideas in order to improve their Web-based materials. Students, in essence, were involved in solving a design task, considered one of the most complex and ill-structured types of problems (Jonassen 1997; Kitchener 1983).

The online discussion ran for 2 weeks, after which the individual student wrote a reflection which included: (a) general comments on the use of asynchronous online discussion; (b) their learning points from facilitation of their own forum; (c) their learning points from observations on how other students facilitated their forums; and (d) their rationale for accepting or rejecting the suggestions or

Table 5.2 Characteristics of Studies 2, 3, and 4

Characteristic	Study 2 (n = 16)	Case 2 (n = 56)	Case 3 (n = 10)
Mode of learning	Blended with face-to-face and online components	Blended with face-to-face and online components	Blended with face-to-face and online components
Discipline of study	Education	Education	Non-education
Type of online component	Peer-facilitated asynchronous online discussion	Peer-facilitated asynchronous online discussion	Peer-facilitated asynchronous online discussion
Online task	Design tasks	Design tasks, dilemma discussion	Design tasks
Duration of online discussion	2 weeks long	4 weeks long	13 weeks long
Discussion requirement	Course credits given for contribution in the discussion; however, no number of posting quota or deadline imposed. Students were free to post in whichever forums they wished.	Course credits given for contribution in the discussion; however, no number of posting quota or deadline imposed. Students were free to post in whichever forums they wished.	Course credits given for contribution in the discussion; however, no number of posting quota or deadline imposed. Students were free to post in whichever forums they wished.
Profile of students	Full-time diploma students (no bachelor degrees yet)	Full-time graduate students	Full-time undergraduate students
Data sources	Student questionnaire, interviews	Student questionnaire, reflections, interviews	Student reflections

comments made by other students on their own design projects. Although course credits were given for contribution in the discussion, students had the freedom to choose to contribute in whichever thread or respond to whom they wished. There was no quota imposed on the number of posts made (e.g. students have to post at least two messages), and no discussion deadline was imposed.

Following the completion of the reflection, a questionnaire survey was conducted. The questionnaire allowed the students to indicate more than one reason as to why they chose to contribute or not contribute to the discussions. Fifteen students completed the questionnaire. Six students were also randomly selected to be interviewed individually to gain more insight into why students chose to contribute in certain discussions but not other forums. Member checking was conducted after the interviews for validity check.

Study 3: Full-Time Diploma in Education Students

Study 3 was carried out in a similar fashion after Study 2. The main difference between Studies 2 and 3 was that the former was a diploma level course while the latter was a graduate level program. The students in Study 3 already had their undergraduate degrees and were pursuing a graduate course in education. The primary research question that was addressed in Study 3 was: What are the motivators and barriers of student online contribution?

Method

A total of 56 students participated in this study. The discussion tasks in Study 3 involved the following: design task and dilemma discussion. With regard to design task, students worked in pairs or in groups of 3–4 to design a multimedia instructional package. After the students had designed the lesson, they uploaded them onto the discussion forums in BlackBoard for peer discussions.

Dilemmas are also ill-structured problems. In dilemmas, there is often no solution that satisfies all people, and there are compromises implicit in every solution (Jonassen 1997). In this study, an ethical dilemma was used. Students were asked to comment on the following topic: "Do you think it is okay for people to buy or sell organs? Justify your opinions." The online discussions were completely facilitated by the students, without involvement from the instructor. Although course credits were also given for contribution in the discussion, students had the freedom to choose to contribute in whichever thread or respond to whom they wished. In addition, no number of posting quota and discussion deadline were imposed.

Data were gathered from the following sources: (a) an end-of-course questionnaire survey, (b) student reflections, and (c) student interviews. The questionnaire measured what students perceived as factors, including facilitation strategies that motivated them to contribute in peer-facilitated discussions. Fifteen students completed the questionnaire. Fourteen students volunteered to be interviewed face-to-face individually for about 30 min each to provide more detailed explanations about some of the motivating factors. Following the interviews, member checking was carried out for validity check. Finally, 41 students completed a student reflection on the following questions: (a) what factors made you contribute in the discussion? (b) what factors discourage you from contributing in the discussion?

Study 4: Full-Time Non Education Undergraduate Students

In the previous Studies 1–3, all the participants involved in the discussions were education major students. We were interested in replicating the previous studies using a different sample of participants. So in Study 4, we had non-education undergraduate students as participants. The same instructor, who oversaw Studies 1–3, was responsible for study 4 to minimize the risk of confounding variable due to possibility of different instructors setting different online activities.

Method

Ten students who majored in disciplines such as business, science, and engineering participated in the study. Study 4 was a blended course that involved both face-to-face lessons and online activity. During the face-to-face lessons, the instructor presented new content materials, and asked students questions to help them recall prior related learning, as well as to assess students' understandings of the current topic. The nature of the online activity was similar to Studies 1–3, that is to design Web-based instructional packages. Each of the 10 students was given an individual discussion forum to upload their design drafts. The students facilitated their own discussion forums to discuss ideas in order to improve their Web-based materials. At the end of the course, students were asked to write a reflection guided by the following questions: "What factors encourage you to participate in other people's forums?", and "What factors discourage you from participating in other students' forums?" Students' reflection data were analyzed using Lincoln and Guba's (1985) constant-comparative method to derive categories relevant to the research objective.

Main Findings of Studies 2, 3, And 4

In this section, we highlight the following four major findings gathered from the aforementioned three studies with regard to other possible ways of increasing student contribution in peer-facilitated online discussions.

5.2.1 Emphasize Efforts to Nurture Relational Capital Among Students

Efforts to establish relational capital is essential. Relational capital refers to personal relationships (e.g., friendships) that people have with each other (Granovetter 1992). Relational capital helps build shared understandings and community feelings, both of which can increase the likelihood of student contribution in online discussions (Hewitt 2005).

As many as 93 % of students in Study 2 reported that they chose to contribute in forums facilitated by peers whom they were familiar with. Similarly, familiarity with peer facilitator was identified as one of the top five reasons why students in Study 3 chose to contribute. As remarked by Kenny, a participant, "I participate if the discussions are facilitated by my friends." This was echoed by Lee, another participant, who stated, "If I knew the facilitator personally, I would be more inclined to participate in that forum. I would be more willing to give my honest opinion as I know that my friend would be able to take my comments and criticisms."

Students tend to avoid interacting with someone whom they are unfamiliar with for fear of offending him or her, particularly if they perceive that the person is not receptive to negative comments. For example, Seng, a participant, stated, "I hesitate to contribute if I don't know the person well because I don't know how he or she might react to my comments."

Since establishing relational capital is important, instructors should focus their attention on helping students to know one another prior to the actual online discussion activity, instead of asking students to do the actual discussion immediately, especially if the students are new to one another. Agre (1998) suggests that individuals need to meet in person, and eat and drink as a group in order to develop shared understandings and community feelings. Instructors should, perhaps, even encourage some off-task talk among participants. Off-task talk plays an important socialization role in online discussions because it can create a sense of shared meaning (Hara 2009), and a sense of familiarity.

Students' familiarity with one another could also positively influence the social presence in an asynchronous online discussion environment (Cheung et al. 2008). Essentially, social presence refers to the perception that there is another real person (instead of merely a name) taking part in the discussion (Short et al. 1976; Tu and McIsaac 2003; Wise et al. 2004). Research has suggested that participants with high social presence tend to post messages that are twice as long as those with low social presence (Wise et al. 2004).

In addition, interview data from Studies 2 and 3 suggested that another possible way to help foster relational capital would be to acknowledge or appreciate the contribution made by people. For example, Koh, a participant, commented, "It[acknowledgement] positively reinforces me to contribute because it affirms that my opinions are worthwhile. I think people generally like to be acknowledged for their contributions." However, such acknowledgement has to be sincere because it may fail to motivate individuals to contribute if the acknowledgement appeared insincere. As Dave, a participant, explained:

> Some peer facilitators merely said 'thank you' or 'thank you for your postings' to every participant who contributed. They did not further elaborate how and why the contributions were useful to them. Such forms of acknowledgement appeared to be a mere formality or lip service to me rather than a sincere gesture.

5.2.2 Remind Students to "Help Other People First"

Individuals usually feel that it is only fair to help others such as contributing ideas and suggestions when they have received help from others in the past (Wasko and Faraj 2000). Such mutual obligation may be referred to as reciprocity, which is the "act of giving benefits to another in return for benefits received" (Molm et al. 2007, p. 200). Becker (1956, p. 1) referred the human species as "homo reciprocus", Gouldner (1960) noted that a norm of reciprocity helps ensure that people help others who have helped them before, while Nowak and Sigmund (2000, p. 819) described reciprocity as shrewd investments where "we give to receive".

Reciprocity may be either direct or indirect (Nowak and Sigmund 2000). In direct reciprocity, the recipient of a benefit or help returns a benefit directly to the giver, while in indirect reciprocity, the recipient does not return a benefit directly to the giver but to other people in the social circle (Molm et al. 2007). Specifically, the analysis of the interview data from Studies 2 and 3 suggested that students in our studies received help from the same individual they helped before, that is direct reciprocity. For example, Kenny, a participant, explained, "When I noticed that Dave responded frequently to my postings as well as other people's postings in my discussion forum, I felt that it was only morally right that I went and do the same in his discussions too." This was echoed by Krista, a participant in Study 4, who wrote:

> In addition, I tend to participate more in forums of specific individuals who also contributed to my forum. I like the sort of dependency between me and the other party in situations like this. The reciprocal relationship between me and the other party assured me that my thoughts are valued, and that the other person was willing to share his/her views too. As a result, a form of trust was built. This significantly boosted my confidence to voice out my thoughts comfortably and kept me going back to the forums.

Our finding thus suggested that students should first help others (e.g., contribute ideas). When they do so, it is likely that this will motivate other students to reciprocate by contributing in return. Although this may merely be a transactional exchange at the beginning, the results of reciprocity tend to forge relationships that will grow in trust and increase the relational capital among individuals over time (Uzzi 1996).

It is important to note that at the initial stage, individuals usually exchange help based on the instrumental or utilitarian value of the initial help provided (Molm et al. 2007). In other words, if the initial help rendered is of superficial value (e.g., one-liner postings with no elaboration), there is a high chance the recipient would be put off from contributing in return (Hew et al. 2010a, b). For example, Goh, a participant, explained:

> When I realize that people in the forum are talking crap or making arguments merely for the sake of making them, I stop contributing. I think it's a complete waste of time when people do not think through their points and post their comments for the sake of having something in the forum. It irks me!

As the examples above illustrate, reciprocity is contingent on evidence of trustworthiness such as the soundness of ideas, at least at its initial stages. As such, instructors should remind students to contribute information that is valid and reliable to the best of their ability. This will then increase the chances of the recipients reciprocating the favor.

5.2.3 Choose Interesting Discussion Topics or Questions, Especially Those That are Relevant and Controversial

It is widely acknowledged that the choice of the discussion topic or question plays a vital role in determining the success of an online discussion. However, what exactly entails an appropriate topic or question may not be entirely clear. Our findings from Studies 2, 3, and 4 suggested two major dimensions that make a topic or question interesting to motivate students to contribute in a peer-facilitated discussion environment.

First, topics that are interesting to students are topics that directly concern or relate to the students' own subject matter or personal experience. For example, Chew, a participant, explained:

> I was enticed to forums which had interesting topics which I could relate to. One example was the discussion on the use of Facebook. I had always used Facebook as a social medium to connect with my friends. Thus the topic of Facebook got me all excited because it was directly related to my personal experiences. I find the topic easy to talk about, and I could generate more ideas.

Another participant, Andy, remarked, "The topics that interest me are topics that are relevant to me. By relevant, I mean that these are topics that I could apply to my own project." When asked to explain why the relevance of a discussion topic is important, students explain that they had the knowledge to share in such topics as compared to irrelevant topics. For example, Sandy, a participant, stated, "I did not contribute in some of the discussions because I don't know the content or subject being discussed well."

Second, topics or questions that are interesting to students are those that are controversial in nature. Controversial topics are open-ended, with many possible answers depending on the assumptions that a student makes. Such topics or questions lend themselves very well to conflict of ideas which could spur people to respond. For example, Chee, a participant, remarked, "Conflict of ideas provides room for discussion and debate, especially when the data proves counter to what many people think."

5.2.4 Peer Facilitators Should Periodically Summarize the Main Points of a Discussion and Follow Up with Relevant Questions After the Summary

Finally, peer facilitators should summarize the main points of a discussion thread when the thread contains many postings. Results of our studies suggested that summarizing the major ideas serves two major purposes.

First, it prevents information overload on the part of the readers because students can quickly get a gist of what the postings are about by simply reading the summary instead of having to plow through every single contribution made. Students tend to stop contributing in a discussion if it contains many messages. For example, Loh, a participant, explained, "It was very mentally exhausting to go through each message in a forum and post a comment. Eventually, I ended up with only commenting to a few messages due to an exhaustion of the mind."

Second, it helps students to keep track of the discussion in order to respond appropriately, in order to avoid further repetitions of the same issues. For example, Liz, a participant, stated, "Reading a summary helps me to easily identify what others have said so far in the discussion so that I know exactly what else I can contribute."

So far, we have addressed the need for summarizing. It is also important to address the issue of what to do *after* summarizing the main points of a discussion. Our studies found that not all students agreed that having a summary of the main points of a discussion thread motivated them to contribution to the discussion. Providing a summary may unwittingly end a discussion. The students explained that the posting of a summary suggested that the peer facilitator had made a decision on whose and which views to take up. Hence, other participants stopped contributing because they felt as if the discussion had been concluded. As Mark, a participant, explained, "Giving a summary or closure suggests to me that no further discussion is needed. It tells me that I don't need to contribute anymore even if I have something to say." To encounter this problem, some participants recommended that peer facilitators follow up with questions (e.g., questions that ask people for further comments if they have any), or suggest new directions for discussion after the summary.

References

Agre, P. (1998). Networking on the network. *Crosswords, 4*(4), 14–21.

Becker, H. P. (1956). *Man in reciprocity*. New York: Praeger.

Cheung, W. S., Hew, K. F., & Ng, S. L. C. (2008). Toward an understanding of why students contribute in asynchronous online discussions. *Journal of Educational Computing Research, 38*(1), 29–50.

Costa, A. L. (2000). Describing the habits of mind. In A. L. Costa & B. Kallick (Eds.), *Book 1: Discovering and exploring habits of mind* (pp. 21–40). Alexandria: Association for Supervision and Curriculum Department.

Costa, A. L., & Kallick, B. (2000). Assessing the Habits of Mind. In A. L. Costa & B. Kallick (Eds.), *Book 3: Assessing and reporting on habits of mind* (pp. 29–53). Alexandria: Association for Supervision and Curriculum Development.

Dewey, J. (1933). *How we think: A restatement of the relation of reflective thinking to the education process*. New York: D. C. Heath.

Ennis, R. H. (1987). A taxonomy of critical thinking dispositions and abilities. In J. B. Baron & R. S. Sternberg (Eds.), *Teaching thinking skills: Theory and practice* (pp. 9–26). New York: W. H. Freeman.

Facione, P. A., Sanchez, C. A., Facione, N. C., & Gainen, J. (1995). The disposition toward critical thinking. *Journal of General Education, 44*(1), 1–25.

Gouldner, A. W. (1960). The norm of reciprocity: A preliminary statement. *American Sociological Review, 25*, 161–178.

Granovetter, M. S. (1992). Problems of explanation in economic sociology. In N. Nohria & R. Eccles (Eds.), *Networks and organizations: Structure, form and action* (pp. 25–56). Boston, MA: Harvard Business School Press.

Hara, N. (2009). *Communities of practice: Fostering peer-to-peer learning and informal knowledge sharing in the workplace*. Berlin: Springer.

Hew, K. F., & Cheung, W. S. (2009). Participation in student-facilitated discussion forums: An empirical analysis of facilitators' habits of mind. In B. H. Tan & S. R. Galea (Eds.), *Proceedings of the 14th International Conference on Thinking 2009* (pp. 268–279). Kuala Lumpur: Universiti Putra Malaysia.

Hew, K. F., Cheung, W. S., & Jumain, S. N. (2010a). Critical thinking in asynchronous online discussions: Examining the role of the student facilitator. In Z. Abas, et al. (Eds.),

Proceedings of Global Learn Asia Pacific 2010 (pp. 4210–4215). Chesapeake: Association for the Advancement of Computing in Education.

Hew, K. F., Cheung, W. S., & Ng, C. S. L. (2010b). Student contribution in asynchronous online discussion: A review of the research and empirical exploration. *Instructional Science, 38*(6), 571–606.

Hew, K. F., & Cheung, W. S. (2011b). Student facilitators' habits of mind and their influences on higher-level knowledge construction occurrences in online discussions: A case study. *Innovations in Education and Teaching International, 48*(3), 275–285.

Hewitt, J. (2005). Toward an understanding of how threads die in asynchronous computer conferences. *Journal of the Learning Sciences, 14*(4), 567–589.

Jonassen, D. H. (1997). Instructional design models for well-structured and ill-structured problem solving learning outcomes. *Educational Technology Research and Development, 45*(1), 65–94.

Kitchener, K. S. (1983). Cognition, metacognition, and epistemic cognition: A three-level model of cognitive processing. *Human Development, 26*, 222–232.

Lincoln, Y. S., & Guba, E. G. (1985). *Naturalistic inquiry*. Beverly Hills: Sage Publications.

Marzano, R. J., Pickering, D. J., & McTighe, J. (1993). *Assessing student outcomes: Performance assessment using the dimensions of learning model.* Alexandria: Association for Supervision and Curriculum Development.

Molm, L. D., Schaefer, D. R., & Collett, J. L. (2007). The value of reciprocity. *Social Psychology Quarterly, 70*(2), 199–217.

Neo, C. E., & Cheung, W. S. (2007). A framework for enculturating thinking dispositions. *The Korean Journal of Thinking and Problem Solving, 17*(2), 67–76.

Nowak, M. A., & Sigmund, K. (2000). Shrewd investments. *Science, 288*, 819–820.

Short, J., Williams, E., & Christie, B. (1976). *The social psychology of telecommunications*. New York: Wiley.

Tishman, S. (2000). Why teach habits of mind? In A. L. Costa & B. Kallick (Eds.), *Habits of mind: A developmental series* (pp. 41–52). Alexandria: Association for Supervision and Curriculum Development.

Tishman, S., Perkins, D. N., & Jay, E. (1995). *The thinking classroom: Learning and teaching in a culture of thinking*. USA: Allyn & Bacon.

Tu, C.-H., & McIsaac, M. (2002). The relationship of social presence and interaction in online classes. *The American Journal of Distance Education, 16*(3), 131–150.

Uzzi, B. (1996). The sources and consequences of embeddedness for the economic performance of organizations: The network effect. *American Sociological Review, 61*, 674–698.

Wasko, M. M., & Faraj, S. (2000). "It is what one does:" Why people participate and help others in electronic communities of practice. *Journal of Strategic Information Systems, 9*, 155–173.

Wise, A., Chang, J., Duffy, T., & del Valle, R. (2004). The effects of teacher social presence on student satisfaction, engagement, and learning. *Journal of Educational Computing Research, 31*(3), 247–271.

Chapter 6
Case Studies on Peer Facilitation: How to Sustain Participants' Online Discussion?

In the previous chapter, we highlighted several findings on some possible ways to increase student contribution in peer facilitated online discussions. However, another question that should also be asked is what makes an online discussion sustainable. To address this question, we conducted the following three studies that examined the growth of discussion threads. The first study examined thread development patterns, while the other two studies examined, in greater detail, the role of questions as well as other facilitation techniques that could foster the continuity of threaded discussion over time.

We are interested in studying thread sustainability because of the relationship of online discussion threads to social constructivist learning (Hewitt 2005). The social constructivist learning perspective suggests that individuals learn by exchanging ideas or opinions with one another. In order for this to take place, sustained online discussion, typically characterized by long threads, should ideally be the norm because it typically takes many exchanges of postings for students to share viewpoints, explore different perspectives, negotiate issues, and create mutual understandings (Guzdial and Turns 2000; Hewitt 2005).

6.1 Examining Thread Development Patterns

Study 5

Study 5 was conducted to address the following two major research questions (Chan et al. 2009): (a) what patterns characterize the growth of AOD threads? (b) how does the practice of peer-facilitation techniques affect thread development?

Method

The context of study was a graduate level (Master) course entitled *Designing Asynchronous Online Discussion*. This course introduced students to the advantages and disadvantages of using asynchronous discussion as an instructional strategy, the

K. F. Hew and W. S. Cheung, *Student Participation in Online Discussions*,
DOI: 10.1007/978-1-4614-2370-6_6, © Springer Science+Business Media, New York 2012

principles of designing asynchronous discussion, as well as methods of facilitating and evaluating the discussion. Fourteen students initially attended the course. One student, however, dropped the course due to work commitment soon after it began.

Each student was required to design a lesson incorporating the use of asynchronous discussion. Each student was given his or her own discussion forum in BlackBoard. After the students had designed their lesson plans, they posted them in their respective forums. Each student became the owner and facilitator of his or her own discussion forum. The forums provided students the opportunity to give comments, suggestions, or ask questions about each other's lesson plan. Altogether, the online discussion ran for 3 weeks. Data were gathered from students' discussion posts, reflections, and interviews.

Students' discussion posts were examined to identify the growth pattern of discussion threads. Discussion forums with a higher number of postings were selected because such forums would most probably show the growth patterns of thread over time as compared to forums with no or few postings. Since the mean number of postings per student for the class was 21.2, only those discussion forums with more than 21 postings were selected and the structure of the threads was examined. Content analysis was used to analyze how the practice of facilitation techniques shaped the growth patterns of threads over time. Two raters coded the student facilitators' techniques separately. Any discrepancies of the coding were discussed and negotiated until a 100 % mutual agreement was reached.

Main Findings of Study 5

An examination of the growth patterns of threads over time pointed to three typical thread patterns: short thread pattern, extended thread pattern, and split thread pattern (see Fig. 6.1).

A short thread pattern suggests that a sustained discussion is not taking place because it contains only two postings—the starter note and a reply to the starter. The formation of an extended thread pattern, on the other hand, typically suggests that peer facilitators and participants are engaged in a sustained discussion involving a single idea or issue within a particular discussion topic. The formation of a split thread pattern also suggests that the facilitators and participants are engaged in a sustained discussion but they are involved in two or more ideas or issues that are posted in at least two subthreads. Further analysis of the data suggested the following findings.

6.1.1 The Mere Number of Peer Facilitator Postings Appears to Have No Influence. Also Avoid Trying To Resolve Differences Early

The mere number of peer facilitators' postings per se did *not* necessarily have the effect of sustaining the online discussion. We also found that lengthy messages tend to dissuade people from continuing a discussion. For example, an examination of peer facilitator Gwen's postings revealed that Gwen's messages tended to

Short Thread Pattern:

Post 1:
- Post 2:

(no more than 2 posts)

Extended Thread Pattern:

Post 1:
- Post 2:
  - Post 3:
    - Post 4:

(3 or more posts; each post building on preceding post)

Split Thread Pattern:

Post 1:
- Post 2:
  - Post 3: **(split post from note 2)**
    - Post 5:
      - Post 7: **(split post from note 5)**
        - Post 10:
          - Post 13:
        - Post 11:
          - Post 14:
      - Post 8: **(split post from note 5)**
        - Post 12:
          - Post 15:
  - Post 4: **(split post from note 2)**
    - Post 6:
      - Post 9:

Fig. 6.1 Types of thread pattern

be too lengthy (e.g., mostly about two-thirds of a page for each reply to other participants), suggesting that this might have discouraged other participants from reading and responding in return. Results also suggest that peer facilitators who attempt to resolve differences and conflicts in opinions early in the discussion tend to foster thread termination because it signals to other participants that a decision has been made and thus further discussions are not necessary. On the other hand, the application of questioning technique appears to continue the discussion most of the time.

6.2 Investigating the Role of Questions and Other Facilitation Techniques

From Study 5, we learned that the use of questions appear to promote thread continuity. However, Study 5 did not elaborate on the types of questions and how they might affect thread sustainability. We therefore conducted two additional studies to examine the role of questions in greater detail, as well as other facilitation techniques that could sustain an online discussion. Table 6.1 provides a summary of the two studies. Each of the two studies will be described first, followed by a cross-case discussion of the main findings.

Study 6

The purpose of Study 6 was to examine the facilitation techniques employed by peer facilitators to sustain an online discussion (Hew & Cheung, 2008).

Method

Twenty-four students, who were enrolled in a post-diploma course in Instructional Technology, participated in the study. The course was a blended one involving face-to-face and asynchronous online discussion sections. All 24 students had the opportunity to be facilitators and participants in the online discussion. Three topics of online discussion were discussed, each topic lasting one week. The first topic of discussion was "How can teachers implement information technology tools to engage student learning?" The second topic of discussion was "How can information technology tools be used to facilitate problem-based learning?" The third topic focused on "How technology tools can be used to address different students' learning styles?"

There were four groups of students, with six members each, in each discussion topic. In each topic of discussion, the students were randomly assigned into the four groups and two students were randomly chosen as peer facilitators. Students who served as facilitators before would not be chosen as facilitators again. After the online discussions had ended, each student wrote a reflection which required them to: (a) state four facilitation skills that they used in the online forum and explain why they applied them in those instances, and (b) identify three different facilitation skills that students learned from their peers.

Students' online posts were examined to identify the extent to which the discussions were sustained. We considered a thread to have a sustained discussion if it had a depth of at least six levels of message posted (see Fig. 6.2).

Content analysis was used to analyze the peer facilitators' online posts to examine the facilitation techniques used. Specifically, the online posts were examined via the constant-comparative method to build emergent and initial data categories of facilitation techniques (Lincoln and Guba, 1985). The inter-rater reliability of the coding was 92 %.

Study 7

In order to further explore the research question on what factors may sustain student discussion in peer-facilitated online forums, as well as to confirm the findings in Study 6 we carried out Study 7 (Ng et al. 2009). Sustained discussion is defined in this study as discussion threads which are at least three levels deep.

Method

The context of Study 7 was a graduate level course which introduced students to the principles of effective multimedia design. Sixteen students attended the course. The multimedia course was an intensive one that was conducted over 4 full

Table 6.1 Characteristics of Studies 6 and 7

Characteristic	Study 6 ($n = 24$)	Study 7 ($n = 16$)
Mode of learning	Blended with face-to-face and online components	Blended with face-to-face and online components
Discipline of study	Education	Technology (multimedia design)
Type of online component	Peer-facilitated asynchronous online discussion	Peer-facilitated asynchronous online discussion
Online task	Discussion task (3 topics)	Design task
Duration of online discussion	3 Weeks long	4 Weeks long
Discussion requirement	Course credits given for contribution in the discussion; however, no number of posting quota or deadline imposed. Students randomly grouped into four groups of six members each, each handling a specific discussion topic.	Students were not given any credits for their postings. No number of posting quota or deadline imposed. Students were free to post in whichever forums they wished.
Profile of students	Full-time post-diploma students	Part-time graduate students
Data sources	Online posts	Online posts, questionnaire, interviews

days. The first 3 days were held on consecutively, while the last day of the course was held one month later. During the first 3 days, students were taught multimedia principles and concepts and worked with a partner to come up with a draft project proposal and storyboard for a multimedia product. The students then uploaded their project proposal and storyboard to an online discussion forum after the third lesson.

The instructor created one discussion forum for each pair of students to upload their project proposal and storyboard for peer critique. The students facilitated their own forum and received feedback to improve their project plan and storyboard. Although the students worked in pairs, only one of them facilitated the forum. It was up to the pair to appoint who the facilitator should be. This meant that 8 out of the 16 students in the course were peer facilitators and hence there was a total of eight peer facilitated asynchronous online discussions for this study. However, all students in the course were expected to participate in all the other discussion forums. The students had the freedom to choose to contribute in whichever discussion forums they wished. The asynchronous online discussions ran for about 4 weeks. The students were not given any grades for their postings in the asynchronous online discussion. Data were gathered from students' discussion posts, questionnaires, and interviews.

Thread	Author
Engaging student with online forum:	HLT
RE: Engaging student with online forum:	SH
RE: Engaging student with online forum:	SSI
RE: Engaging student with online forum:	TH
RE: Engaging student with online forum:	CWS
RE: Engaging student with online forum:	CL

Fig. 6.2 An example of a six-level deep discussion thread

Main Findings of Studies 6 and 7

In this section, we offer the following four major findings from the aforementioned Studies 6 and 7 with regard to the possible ways of sustaining student contribution in peer facilitated online discussions.

6.2.1 The Use of Questions Appears to Sustain the Discussion

The earlier results from Study 5 suggested that the mere number of peer facilitator's postings per se did *not* necessarily have the effect of sustaining the online discussion. On the other hand, the application of questioning technique appears to continue the discussion. Specifically, what types of questions are useful? Based on the results of Study 6, two types of questions appear to foster seven- or more-level deep threads: (a) questions about other people's opinions, and (b) questions of clarification. An example of the former is, "Do you think it is feasible to use ICT tools to teaching attitude change?" "If yes, how can it be done?" An example of a question of clarification is, "In your previous post, you mentioned that you drew the images on Paint and put them together. Can you clarify, would it be a static single scene, or did you intend to come up with a movie clip?" Asking questions of clarification helps to clear up ambiguous points, keep the discussion focused, and assures participants that they are on the right track which gives them more confidence to continue to contribute.

In addition, Study 6 suggested that questions should be posed toward the end of a post rather than in front. Posing questions *later* rather than earlier appears to foster a greater sense of obligation on the part of the participants to reply to the questions; hence increasing the odds of sustaining a discussion.

6.2.2 Encourage Peer Facilitators to Convey Sincere Appreciation for Other People's Contribution

Showing appreciation for other people's contributions appears to *both* encourage individuals to contribute as well as sustain a discussion. However, as noted in the previous chapter, participants have to show sincerity in their appreciation. In Study 6, we found that showing sincere appreciation may foster seven-level deep threads which suggest the possibility that the discussion is sustained or extended. A representative example is, "Thanks H for your concise and quick response. Your comments made me reconsider my prior assumption about the target audience, which may not be entirely valid."

Analysis of the data revealed that showing appreciation attracted and sustained student contribution in a discussion because it made students feel that they were worthy contributors; that their contributions were deemed important enough to be noticed. For example, Ashley, a participant explained, "Acknowledging participants' contribution aids in encouraging discussions as it ensures that the participants of the forum obtain the satisfaction that their views have been taken note of and this fosters further discussion". This was echoed by another participant, Nick, who explained:

> The student facilitator's posts tended to start off with a brief appreciation to individuals who contributed. This, I felt, led to a general feeling of infectious warmth within the forum and a subsequent desire to share even more. This uplifting and encouraging tone could be the main contributory factor to why I was the most active participant in the discussion.

6.2.3 Refrain from Citing Sources Too Often

To sustain discussion, participants should perhaps refrain from citing or quoting sources too often to support their initial ideas. In Study 7, we found that citing sources too often could be interpreted by other participants to mean that further suggestions are not welcome because it sounds condescending. For example, Wong, a participant, explained, "I tend to respond to questions which ask for opinions, rather than to those that quote certain sources of experts. For example, according to so-and-so, it should be " Another participant, Soh, remarked, "If the person quotes from somewhere very often, it sounds condescending."

6.2.4 Show Openness to Feedback

One way to show openness to feedback is to explicitly encourage participants to contribute. There are two ways by which this could be done: (a) general invitation, and (b) personal invitation. In the former, a message is posted to all participants inviting them to contribute in the discussion. A representative example would be, "Dear/Hi all would appreciate your thoughts about this plan/issue." When a peer facilitator encourages people to contribute, the participants generally feel that he or she is open to their suggestions and welcome feedback. For example, Kathy, a participant, said, "When the facilitator encourages all members to participate, I feel that he/she welcomes feedback and is open for comments."

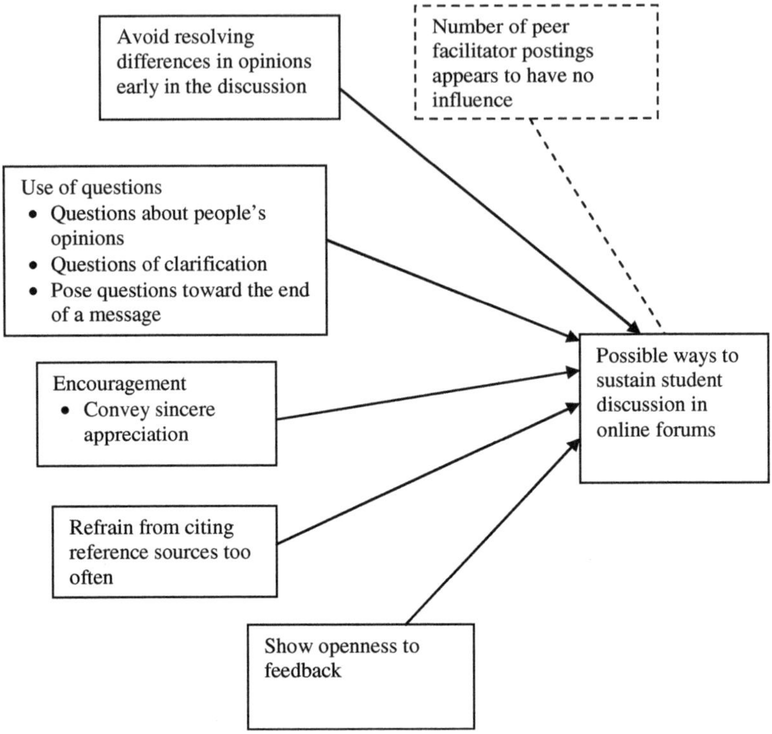

Fig. 6.3 Major findings regarding possible ways to sustain student discussion

On the other hand, some peer facilitators may specifically invite certain individuals to contribute. For example, "Hi G and E, could you share your views on this issue?" John, a participant, explained, "If the facilitator personally invites me, by name in asynchronous online discussion, I feel obliged to help."

However, it is important to note that while this strategy could encourage contribution from certain participants, it could backfire and put off others whose names are not stated in the online post. For example, Cindy, a participant shared, "When the facilitator addresses his responses to the one who posts the message, I'm sometimes not sure if I should come in and answer. I feel that I am intruding into their discussion."Another participant gave hint to a possible solution to overcome this problem. This participant, Koh, mentioned that if the peer facilitator ended his posting with "What about the rest", he would try to contribute because this signaled that comments and feedback from other participants were welcomed as well. Another possible solution is to send personal e-mails or short messages (SMS) via phone directly to specific participants to invite them to contribute.

Recipients should also show openness to feedback by suspending judgment and not harshly criticize or put down any ideas. An individual's contribution such as ideas and comments is a very important component of his or her self-efficacy and personal self-image (Wasko and Faraj, 2000). Refraining from harsh criticism helps reduce the possibility that an individual student's personal self-image is being threatened because attacks on an individual's contribution, which are typically viewed as attacks on the individual itself and destroys future contribution, are minimized.

Figure 6.3 summarizes the major findings of Studies 5, 6, and 7 on some possible ways to sustain student discussion in online forums.

References

Chan, C. C., Hew, K. F., & Cheung, W. S. (2009). Asynchronous online discussion thread development: Examining growth patterns and peer-facilitation techniques. *Journal of Computer Assisted Learning, 25*(5), 438–452.

Hewitt, J. (2005). Toward an understanding of how threads die in asynchronous computer conferences. *Journal of the Learning Sciences, 14*(4), 567–589.

Guzdial, M., & Turns, J. (2000). Effective discussion through a computer-mediated anchored forum. *Journal of the Learning Sciences, 9*(4), 437–469.

Hew, K. F., & Cheung, W. S. (2008). Attracting student participation in asynchronous online discussions: A case study of peer facilitation. *Computers & Education, 51*, 1111–1124.

Lincoln, Y. S., & Guba, E. G. (1985). *Naturalistic inquiry*. Beverly Hills: Sage Publications.

Ng, C. S. L., Cheung, W. S., & Hew, K. F. (2009). Sustaining asynchronous online discussions: Contributing factors and peer facilitation techniques. *Journal of Educational Computing Research, 41*(4), 477–511.

Wasko, M. M., & Faraj, S. (2000). "It is what one does:" Why people participate and help others in electronic communities of practice. *Journal of Strategic Information Systems, 9*, 155–173.

References

Chapter 7
Case Studies on Peer Facilitation: How to Foster Higher Levels of Knowledge Construction

Up to this point, our focus has been on studies that examined possible ways to increase student contribution as well as sustain online discussions in peer facilitated forums. In this chapter, we would like to focus on possible ways that can foster higher knowledge construction levels. However, before we do that, it will be helpful to revisit what we mean by knowledge, as well as higher knowledge construction levels in this book. We consider knowledge as referring to information, procedures, facts, opinions, experiences, or ideas (Alavi and Leider 1999, 2001). This definition is consistent with the applied perspective of knowledge (Hew and Hara 2007).

We define higher levels of knowledge construction as the sum of the frequency of level II (exploration of dissonance, disagreement), level III (negotiation of meaning), level IV (testing and modification), and level V (application of negotiated ideas, and students' self-reflective statement of new knowledge construction) occurrences as measured by Gunawardena et al. (1997) interaction analysis model.

Although there are several different models that examine the levels of knowledge construction (De Wever et al. 2006), we decided to adopt Gunawardena et al. (1997) model because this particular model focuses on the "overall pattern of knowledge construction emerging from a conference, and is a relatively straightforward scheme" (Lally 2001, p. 402). It is also considered a relatively reliable and straightforward scheme (Lally 2001; Marra et al. 2004).

7.1 Investigating the Role of Group Size, Duration of Discussion, and Peer Facilitation Techniques

In this section, we describe and summarize the main findings of three studies. The first study examined the possible relationship between the frequency of higher level knowledge construction occurrences and group size, while the other two studies examined, the role of peer facilitation techniques, as well as the duration of

K. F. Hew and W. S. Cheung, *Student Participation in Online Discussions*,
DOI: 10.1007/978-1-4614-2370-6_7,

Table 7.1 Characteristics of studies 8, 9, and 10

Characteristic	Study 8 (n = 28 forums)	Study 9 (n = 12 forums)	Study 10 (n = 40 forums)
Mode of learning	Blended with face-to-face and online components	Blended with face-to-face and online components	Blended with face-to-face and online components
Discipline of study	Education, engineering, science, business	Engineering, science, business	Education
Profile of students	Full-time undergraduate and full-time post-diploma students	Full-time undergraduate students	Part-time graduate students, full-time diploma students
Type of online component	Peer-facilitated asynchronous online discussion	Peer-facilitated asynchronous online discussion	Peer-facilitated asynchronous online discussion
Online task	Design task	Design task	Design task
Duration of online discussion	3 weeks	3 weeks	6 weeks
Discussion requirement	Course credits given for contribution in the discussion, no number of posting quota or deadline imposed.	Course credits given for contribution in the discussion, no number of posting quota or deadline imposed	Course credits given for contribution in the discussion, no number of posting quota or deadline imposed
Data sources	Online posts	Online posts, reflections	Online post, interviews, reflections

the online discussion. Table 7.1 provides a summary of these three studies. We describe each study first, followed by a cross-case discussion of the main findings.

Description of Study 8

Study 8 was conducted to answer the following two questions: (a) is there a relationship between the frequency of higher level of knowledge construction occurrences and the group size of discussion forums? and (b) what is the mean group size of the more successful forums versus the less successful forums? (Hew and Cheung, 2010b).

Method

Data were collected from 28 discussions forums. All 28 discussion forums were completely peer facilitated. We referred the group size of an online discussion to the number of people who posted messages in the discussion. Group size of the discussions varied from 1 to 12 people per forum. Students were required to design instructional materials to be used in education or training contexts. They were asked to upload their design projects into their own discussion forums. Students used the discussion forums to identify design problems of their peers' design projects, provide viewpoints for improvements, and respond to the comments raised. Students' online postings were coded in order to establish the levels of knowledge construction. Overall percent agreement of the coding was 80.6 %.

Following the completion of the coding, we tabulated the frequency of occurrences for each knowledge construction level in each of the 28 discussion forum. The sum of the frequency of levels II, III, IV, and V occurrences constituted the frequency of higher level knowledge construction. A Pearson product moment correlation coefficient was subsequently computed to examine if a statistically significant relationship existed between group size and the frequency of higher level knowledge construction occurrences.

To address the second question, "what is the mean group size of the more successful forums versus the less successful forums?", we first defined the more successful forums as discussion forums that had greater occurrences of higher knowledge construction levels (i.e., the sum of the frequency of levels II, III, IV, and V). Since the mean number of levels II to V occurrences was 4.75 for the entire 28 forums, we considered forums with 5 or more levels of II to V instances as the more successful forums. Fourteen such forums were found. The remaining 14 forums were considered to be the less successful ones. We then computed the mean group size of the 14 more successful forums. The answer to this question could provide an indication to a certain critical mass, possibly an optimum discussion group size which may be required to direct the discussion to higher levels of knowledge construction.

Description of Study 9

One of the main purposes of study 9 was to examine if certain facilitation techniques might foster higher knowledge construction levels (Hew and Cheung 2010a).

Method

Data were collected from 12 online discussion forums involving undergraduate students. As part of their course assignment, each student designed a project detailing the use of asynchronous online discussion as an instructional strategy within the primary or secondary school context. Students utilized the discussion forums to discuss design problems of their peers' design projects, provide viewpoints or suggestions for improvements, and respond to the comments raised. At the end of the course, the students completed their reflections that explained the facilitation techniques they had used, and how these might help foster higher level knowledge construction in an online discussion environment. Students' online postings were analyzed in order to establish the levels of knowledge construction as well as the types of peer facilitation techniques used in the discussions. The percent agreement of the knowledge construction and facilitation techniques coding were 80.4 and 82.5 %, respectively.

Description of Study 10

In order to further explore the research question on what factors may foster higher levels of knowledge construction in peer-facilitated online forums, as well as to test the findings in the earlier two studies (8 and 9), we conducted Study 10. Altogether, the following three questions were examined: (a) Is there a relationship between group size and the frequency of higher level knowledge construction occurrences? (b) Is there a relationship between the duration of the online discussion and the frequency of higher level knowledge construction occurrences? (c) Are there any differences between forums that have more higher levels of knowledge construction occurrences and those that do not in terms of the types of facilitation techniques used, as well as the frequency in which the techniques were employed? (Hew and Cheung 2011a)

Method

Study 10 was organized into two sections. In the first section, we examined the relationship between higher level knowledge construction and group size, as well as the discussion duration. Data were collected through online observations of 40 peer discussion forums from three courses: course A (January 2007 semester, graduate level such as students pursuing a Masters or doctoral degree) with 12 forums, course B (January 2006 semester, non-graduate level such as students pursuing a diploma certification) with 12 forums, and course C (July 2005 semester, non-graduate level) with 16 forums.

Each discussion forum utilized the same discussion forum, which was the threaded discussion tool available in BlackBoard™. Participants in the online discussions, including the peer facilitators, were education major students. This was to minimize the risk of possible confounding variable due to the involvement of students from other disciplinary areas. The same instructor was overall responsible for the 40 forums. This was to minimize the risk of confounding variables due to the possibility of different online activities employed by different instructors.

All 40 forums had an ill-structured problem solving, specifically design task, as their discussion activity. The purpose of this criterion was to ensure that all forums shared a similar activity or task, so that the influence of group size and duration of the online discussion on knowledge construction (if any) would be easier to identify. The conceptual knowledge base of the design topic (e.g., principles of instructional design) was provided to students before the actual online discussion. Students in these forums were engaged in designing instructional materials for use in the schools or training institutes (e.g., a web-based instructional activity on the subtraction of whole numbers for grade two children). Students utilized the discussion forums to identify and determine the nature of the problems or issues related to their peers' projects, give comments, or develop viable solutions for improvements, and respond (e.g., agree or disagree accompanied by justifications or reasons) to the comments raised.

Group sizes, excluding the peer facilitators, ranged from 2 to 10. The duration of the online discussions ranged from 6 to 41 days. We referred the group size of an online discussion to the number of students (excluding the peer facilitator) who made postings in the discussion. We referred the duration of the online discussion to the period (in number of days) between the first and the final messages posted in the discussion. For example, we deemed the duration of an online discussion to be 19 days if the first and final postings were made on September 1, 2008 and September 20, 2008, respectively. The percent agreement of the knowledge construction coding was 93 %.

In the second section, the types of peer facilitation techniques were examined. A further analysis of the data was carried out. Since the mean number of levels II–V occurrences was 7.86 for the entire 40 forums, forums with eight or more levels II–V were considered to be the more frequent forums in terms of higher knowledge construction levels. Specifically, of the 40 forums, 14 more frequent forums were identified. Fourteen less frequent forums were randomly selected from the remaining forums. The entire peer facilitators' postings in these two groups of forums were examined and coded. The percent agreement of the facilitation technique coding was 90 %. The types, as well as the frequency of facilitation techniques used were subsequently examined to see if any differences occur between these two groups.

7.2 Major Findings of Studies 8, 9, and 10 Regarding Possible Ways to Foster Higher Knowledge Construction Levels

In this section, we offer the following six findings learned (see Fig. 7.1) from the aforementioned three studies with regard to possible ways of fostering higher levels of knowledge construction in peer facilitated online discussions.

7.2.1 Split the Online Discussion Into Groups of About 10 People Each

The results of Studies 8 and 10 showed a significant positive correlation between group size and the frequency of higher level knowledge construction occurrences. This suggests that higher level knowledge constructions (phases II–V) tend to occur in forums that have larger number of participants who made postings in the discussion. Although it may be difficult to predict the number of students required for each discussion, the results of Study 8 suggested that groups of about 10 participants (mean group size) achieved significantly more number of higher knowledge construction levels. This therefore suggests that groups of about 10 participants may be an optimum discussion size that is required to direct the discussion to higher levels of knowledge construction.

Why do groups of 10 exhibit more higher levels of knowledge construction in online discussions? One possible reason is that participants in groups of 10 have access to a wider range of perspectives when compared to participants in smaller groups such as groups of 5 or 6. This provides a greater opportunity for participants in groups of 10 to identify the differences between the contributions, to consider all the opinions, and to negotiate the various meanings of ideas or comments raised, as compared to their counterparts in smaller groups. Such activities would help foster the attainment of advanced levels of knowledge

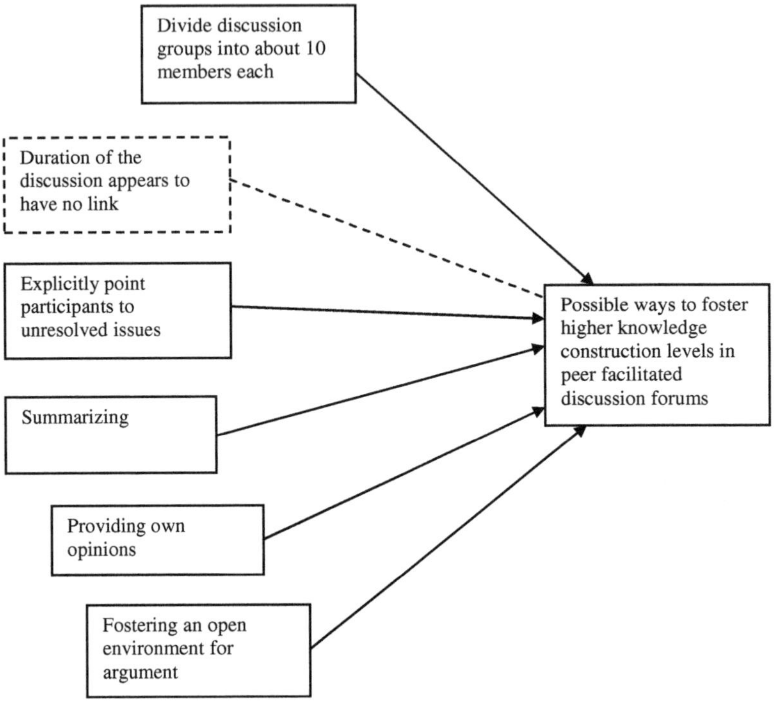

Fig. 7.1 Major lessons learned regarding possible ways to foster higher levels of knowledge construction

construction. It would also be reasonable to expect that discussions in larger groups to reach saturation level much slower than those in smaller groups.

Should we then keep on increasing the group size of a discussion? Most probably not, due to the following two reasons: First, too large a group may encourage the problem of lurking on the part of the participants. Kollock and Smith (1996) described lurkers as free riders, that is noncontributing, resource taking members of a group. Nonnecke and Preece (2000) suggested that as the number of members increases, the need for any given group member to contribute may decline.

Second, too large a group can invoke extraneous cognitive load onto the participants (Schellens and Valcke 2006) as they need to potentially deal with large quantities of postings; this could to reading fatigue, and cause the participants to cease from contributing in the discussion altogether. Our current research finding suggests a group size of about 10 participants may be required to form a critical mass to direct the discussion to higher levels of knowledge construction. However, more work is required to confirm this finding.

7.2.2 Higher Level Knowledge Construction Occurrences Not Linked to the Duration of the Online Discussion

The results of Study 10 revealed no correlation between the duration of online discussion and the frequency of higher level knowledge construction. This is shown by the dotted box and line (without arrow) in Fig. 7.1. This finding is somewhat counterintuitive because one may expect that higher level knowledge construction takes time to form as one needs to read the various opinions posted by others, reflect, and negotiate the different ideas raised. Our finding suggests that merely extending the length of a discussion per se may not be a sufficient condition for higher level knowledge construction to occur. While the precise reason for this is currently unclear, the occurrences of higher knowledge construction levels may be dependent on other host of factors including group size and the facilitation techniques employed by the students in the discussion forums.

7.2.3 Need to Explicitly Point Participants to Unresolved Issues

Results from case study 9 indicated that students in discussion forums that had more higher levels of knowledge construction used the facilitation technique of pointing statistically significantly more frequently than their counterparts in lower-performing forums. Pointing refers to directing the participants of an online discussion in appropriate directions such as by explicitly highlighting unanswered questions, unresolved issues, or differences in opinions. Highlighting unresolved issues could help participants discover and explore disagreements among various viewpoints because it specifically helped participants focus on unresolved issues which they might have otherwise missed or overlooked during the course of the discussion. Candy, one of the participants, stated:

> A participant suggested that I do not give any assessment rubric to students. However, I had a different viewpoint on it. I highlighted this unresolved issue or matter. For example, I commented, 'In that case, does it mean the students would have lesser direction than when they are given a set of rubric?' This helped in exploring the disagreements that we had

Sally, another participant, echoed Candy's reflection:

> It happened when one participant suggested using peer evaluation as a way to assess a student's performance in my lesson. However, another participant felt that it was unnecessary as it would cause distress and pressure amongst the students. I pointed out this unresolved issue and this led to other participants joining in the discussion. In this case, this (pointing) technique worked quite well as the participants gave their suggestions and views. It (pointing) helped people to negotiate the various perspectives, and in the end I was able to come up with a conclusion that peer evaluation should be used in my lesson plan, but not as a major assessment criterion.

We provide the following excerpt (extracted from Hew and Cheung 2010a, pp. 51–52) of an online discussion that developed higher levels of knowledge construction to further illustrate how pointing might be used:

In this particular discussion, participant Y had uploaded his online lesson design plan into the online discussion forum for other participants to critique. In his design plan, participant Y advocated the setting of a ground rule which required secondary two school learners to reply to one another's postings within 24 h.

1. Participant Y: I would prefer a timeframe of 24 h instead of a longer time period for (secondary two) the students to reply. This would be enable students to critically think within that time schedule to ask questions and to post what they learn during class.
2. Participant R: If the discussion is only to span between 1–2 weeks, then 24 h is not too stringent if we want to have a well established online discussion. This is to prevent the posting of only 3–5 replies in the discussion if students are allowed to take their time to reply only within 3 days.
3. Participant C: I disagree. I feel that 24 h is a bit too short. It sort of forces the student to come out with posting under time constraint and the postings may not be of high quality. Why not you set it to be 2 or 3 days? (Highlighting differences of opinions/unresolved issue)
4. Participant Y: (Disagreeing) My stand was that it is for the purpose of students being active learners and receptive of what they learn on the same day, thus allowing them to be more critical when they post their discussion online as compared to a 2–3 day period where their ideas might turn dull.
5. Participant J: To be frank, I really don't think a 24 h rule is feasible because students typically have so many other subjects to study. If you set a 24 h deadline, students may just post very superficial comments which would not help in the discussion. (Highlighting differences of opinions/unresolved issue)
6. Participant Y: Ok. How about if I implement a 48 h rule instead? This is a way to compensate for the different timing we both believe on? The time of 48 h is neither too long nor short for students to post their comments.

In discourse #1 Participant Y shared his rationale for imposing a 24 h rule for students to response to one another in the online forum. This is similar to Gunawardena et al. (1997) phase I which is sharing of opinion. Participant R (#2) shared her agreement of using a 24 h reply (reminiscent of phase I). However, in discourse #3, Participant C countered this claim (reminiscent of phase II, a higher level of knowledge construction: challenging people's ideas, discovering dissonance of opinions). He had a different viewpoint on the ground rule and pointed out that a 24 h reply rule could produce poor replies or comments as students might simply respond due to the pressure of the deadline but not necessarily with serious thoughts or enthusiasm. Participant Y disagreed (#4, phase II) by explaining that learners should be asked to reply within 24 h as the issues under discussion would still remain fresh in their minds. This was again countered by participant J (#5, phase II) who pointed out that students might be overburdened with other school work, and hence not being able to give thoughtful responses within 1 day. The use of the pointing technique to highlight an unresolved issue thus far had led people to giving their various opinions and it helped participant Y negotiate the different perspectives (#6, phase III, a higher level of knowledge construction) and come up with a possible compromise of a 48 h reply rule.

7.2.4 Summarizing

The technique of summarizing may help achieve higher levels of knowledge construction because the summarizers have to first identify the different or contrasting opinions posted in the discussion, then describe which of the contributions hold similar points of view, and finally indicate contradictions and make some provisional conclusions (Schellens et al. 2005). Such tasks or activities relate to higher-level phases such as phase II and III.

7.2.5 Providing Own Opinions

The facilitation technique of providing own comments or opinions may help foster higher-level knowledge constructions in two possible ways. First, providing own opinions helps keep the discussion alive. Thom described it in the following way:

> Due to the lack of physical interactions, participants' contribution may wane during the discussion. It is important [for the peer facilitator] to keep spirits up and encourage discussion from other students by agreeing or disagreeing with their points or sharing personal opinions.

Of course, the activity of keeping a discussion going per se may not guarantee that higher-level knowledge constructions would occur. However, we believe that it is a necessary, if not sufficient, condition for higher-level constructions to take place. If students' contribution in an online discussion wane and eventually stop altogether, the results would be no higher level knowledge constructions at all.

Second, providing own opinions may serve as a starting point to help students in an online discussion move forward to higher-levels of knowledge construction. Schellens et al. (2005) suggested that individuals need a certain amount of such postings before they can move forward to the higher levels of knowledge construction. Schellens et al. (2005) emphasized that a certain number of comments or opinions-related postings are necessary in order to function as a starting point to ground the rest of the online discussion. However, what exactly this number is not ascertained at yet.

7.2.6 Fostering an Open Environment for Argument

Finally, we posit that argumentation or challenging other people's ideas serve as an important starting point to move the discussion forward to higher knowledge construction levels. For example, if no participant in the online discussion is willing to argue or challenge another person's ideas or assumptions, level II (discover of dissonance or disagreement) would not take place. This is similar to Liu et al. (2008) observation that participants in online discussions find it hard to reach higher knowledge construction levels such as the negotiation phase (level III) because they lacked the motivation to challenge or argue with one another.

Typically, in an online discussion, participants are hesitant to challenge other people's ideas because it may be perceived as being confrontational (Liu et al. 2008). Students who wish to challenge other participants' viewpoints may be afraid that their postings be taken negatively by the party that is being challenged which could lead to conflicts—hence they hold back their postings. Therefore, to overcome this problem, it is important to foster an open environment for people to challenge or argue with one another.

Peer facilitators as well as participants could foster an open environment by acknowledging the contributions made by others, including the dissenting viewpoints, as well as encouraging people to contribute. Together such messages help to create a conducive atmosphere for people to discover dissonance and negotiate differing viewpoints.

References

Alavi, M., & Leidner, D. E. (2001). Knowledge Management and knowledge management systems: Conceptual foundations and research issues. *MIS Quarterly, 25*(1), 107–136.

Alavi, M., & Leider, D. E. (1999). Knowledge management systems: Issues, challenges, and benefits. *Communications of the Association for Information Systems, 1*(7), 1–37.

De Wever, B., Schellens, T., Valcke, M., & Van Keer, H. (2006). Content analysis schemes to analyze transcripts of online asynchronous discussion groups: A review. *Computers and Education, 46*, 6–28.

Gunawardena, C. N., Lowe, C. A., & Anderson, T. (1997). Analysis of a global online debate and the development of an interaction analysis model for examining social construction of knowledge in computer conferencing. *Journal Educational Computing Research, 17*(4), 397–431.

Hew, K. F., & Hara, N. (2007). Knowledge sharing in online environments: a qualitative case study. *Journal of the American Society for Information Science and Technology, 59*(14), 2310–2324.

Hew, K. F., & Cheung, W. S. (2010a). Fostering higher knowledge construction levels in online discussion forums: An exploratory case study. *International Journal of Web-based Learning and Teaching Technologies, 5*(4), 44–55.

Hew, K. F., & Cheung, W. S. (2010b). The relationship between group size and advanced level knowledge construction in asynchronous online discussion environments. In C.H. Steel, M.J. Keppell, P. Gerbic & S. Housego (Eds.), Curriculum, technology & transformation for an unknown future. Proceedings ascilite Sydney 2010 (pp.428–432). Sydney.

Hew, K. F., & Cheung, W. S. (2011). Higher-level knowledge construction in asynchronous online discussions: An analysis of group size, duration of online discussion, and student facilitation techniques. *Instructional Science, 39*(3), 303–319.

Kollock, P., & Smith, M. (1996). Managing the virtual commons: cooperation and conflict in computer communities. In S. Herring (Ed.), *Proceeding of Computer-Mediated Communication: Linguistic, social, and cross-cultural perspectives* (pp. 109–128). Amsterdam: John Benjamins.

Lally, V. (2001). Analysing teaching and learning interactions in a networked collaborative learning environment: issues and work in progress. In *Euro CSCL 2001* (pp. 397–405). Retrieved on August 7, 2008 from http://www.ll.unimaas.nl/euro-cscl/Papers/97.doc

Liu, X., Doore, B., & Li, L. (2008). Scaffolding Knowledge Co-Construction in Web-based Discussions through Message Labeling. In K. McFerrin, et al. (Eds.), *Proceedings of Society for Information Technology and Teacher Education International Conference 2008* (pp. 3041–3046). Chesapeake, VA: AACE.

Marra, R., Moore, J., & Klimczak, A. (2004). Content analysis of online discussion forums: a comparative analysis of protocols. *Educational Technology Research and Development, 52*, 23–40.

Nonnecke, B., & Preece, J. (2000). Lurker demographics: counting the silent. In CHI 2000: *Proceedings of the SIGCHI conference on Human factors in computing systems,* pp. 73–80.

Schellens, T., Keer, H. V., & Valcke, M. (2005). The impact of role assignment on knowledge construction in asynchronous discussion groups. *Small Group Research, 36*(6), 704–745.

Schellens, T., & Valcke, M. (2006). Fostering knowledge construction in university students through asynchronous discussion groups. *Computers & Education, 46*, 349–370.

Chapter 8
Peer Versus Instructor: Under What Conditions do Students Prefer?

So far in Chaps. 5–7, we have discussed various findings learned in the context of peer facilitation. However, it is important to note that peer facilitation should not be viewed as a "cure-all" or panacea for all online discussion issues or challenges. In this chapter, we discuss certain conditions or situations that may best be addressed using peer or instructor facilitation. We report the following study in this chapter that attempts to answer this very issue.

8.1 Investigating Peer Versus Instructor Facilitation

Description of study 11:

The purpose of study 11 was to examine the following question: Under what conditions do students prefer peer versus instructor facilitation of an online discussion?

Method:

Altogether 73 participants including full-time undergraduate, diploma, and post-diploma students majoring in different disciplines such as education, engineering, science, and business took part in the study. All 73 participants were enrolled in blended courses with face-to-face tutorials and online discussion activities. The primary source of data was students' completed reflections which were collected at the end of the course. Students were asked to share their view about their facilitator preferences as well as the reasons why they chose such preferences. The students' data were examined by a qualitative coding approach that followed the constant-comparative method of Lincoln and Guba (1985). The students' reflections were examined to classify comments into themes or categories relevant to the research question (i.e., conditions for peer versus instructor facilitation).

K. F. Hew and W. S. Cheung, *Student Participation in Online Discussions*,
DOI: 10.1007/978-1-4614-2370-6_8,

Table 8.1 Peer versus instructor facilitation

Peer facilitation	Instructor facilitation
Participants feel more at ease	Keeping the discussion on topic and set explicit expectations for the discussion
Students taking greater ownership in the discussion	When the topic of discussion is new or profound and requires expert knowledge
Allows practical hands-on experience of being a discussion facilitator	Resolving conflicts in the discussion
Allows greater reflection about other students' ideas in the discussions	

8.2 Major Findings Learned Regarding Conditions or Situations That May Best Be Addressed Using Peer or Instructor Facilitation

We identified three major situations in which students wanted the instructors to act as the facilitator. Table 8.1 summarizes the aforementioned conditions or situations that may best be addressed using peer or instructor facilitation.

8.2.1 Conditions Under Which Students Prefer the Instructor as the Facilitator

First, students preferred the instructor to take care of the organizational matters of the online discussion, particularly to help keep the discussion on topic, and set explicit expectations for the discussion (e.g., deadlines). Students felt that their peers might not command the same kind of moral authority that an instructor had, especially in specifying or setting the directions for discussion. For example, Liza, a participant commented, "I would prefer to have my instructor to facilitate the discussion forum because I would have the assurance that the discussion is going on the right track." Another participant, Lydia, wrote, "Peers may go off topic in the midst of the discussion without them knowing it."

Second, students preferred the instructor to be the facilitator if the topic of discussion is new or profound and requires expert knowledge. In such situations, students felt that an instructor could provide better guidance than peers. For example, Wati, a participant remarked, "My instructor would generally have a higher pool of knowledge and wider range of perspectives about the profound topic, and therefore can provide better and more effective probing questions than my peers could." This was echoed by Jennifer who wrote, "I would prefer my instructor to facilitate the discussion. For example, if a student applies a theory wrongly and the other students do not have the knowledge to point it out, the instructor can rectify the mistake."

Third, students preferred the instructor as a conflict mediator. For example, Ang, a participant explained, "In all discussions, there are bound to be disagreement. Hence, it is important to have someone to resolve the disagreement. It will be more effective if it is done by someone with authority such as the instructor rather than fellow peers." This was echoed by Zhang, another participant, who stated, "The instructor will know what to do when disagreement leads to hostility among different participants. The hostility may reverberate when it is time for face to face lessons or the repercussion may negatively affect the next online discussion".

8.2.2 Conditions Under Which Students Prefer Their Peers as the Facilitator

On the other hand, we identified four situations in which students wanted their peers to act as the facilitator. First, consistent with the findings of prior research, we found that students preferred peer facilitation because they felt more at ease in the online discussion. The following comments illustrate this point: "A discussion forum is a place where I express my viewpoints and share with others. If my instructor is the one facilitating it, it would be harder for me to express my viewpoint and I would think that whatever my instructor say would be right" (Nur, a participant), "Due to the power distance, especially in an Asian culture, students may be more cautious in responding to instructors' questions. Instructors' questions may also risk to be seen as an assessment tool to expose gaps in understanding" (Chew, a participant), and "I feel my peer will be less judgmental of my work. Also, I can easily discuss with him any suggestions or opinions he might have. I will not be able to freely discuss with my instructor in the same manner as he is the one who assess my work. As such there is a tendency for me to agree with my instructor's point of view even if I do not truly agree with it" (Kumar, a participant).

Second, the use of peer facilitation enables students to take greater responsibility and ownership in the discussion. Rather than merely sit back and wait for the instructor's guidance, peer facilitation forces students to take the lead in starting and maintaining the discussion. For example, Lin, a participant, explained, "Assigning students the role of facilitator will allow students to take responsibility and ownership in the success of the discussion and thus they will make an effort to keep the discussion going".

Third, the use of peer facilitation allows students to have actual practical hands-on experience of facilitating an online discussion. Students could practice their facilitation skills, as well as observe and learn from the peers how they facilitate the discussion forums. By doing that, they would have a better understanding of the role of an online discussion facilitator. This was highlighted by Khoo, a participant:

Experiencing what it is like to facilitate your own forum is an essential learning experience for me. By facilitating my own forum, I was able to try out different facilitation techniques and see the different responses to them. I was also able to see how different people facilitate their forums differently and thus learn from a more diverse field of facilitators rather than just the instructor alone.

Fourth, students reported that they reflected more about other students' ideas in the discussions when they acted as peer facilitators than as participants. Perhaps one explanation for this is that peer facilitators tend to read every online post in order to know how to respond to the comments or questions, and summarize the key points that were raised when the number of message postings got large and post the summaries sometime during the online discussions. All these activities push peer facilitators to reflect on their own ideas as well as other students' ideas carefully.

Reference

Lincoln, Y. S., & Guba, E. G. (1985). Naturalistic inquiry. Beverly Hills: Sage Publications.

Chapter 9
Asynchronous Audio Discussion

9.1 Introducing Audio-Based Online Discussion

Almost all asynchronous online discussion environments are currently text-based and require typing skills and a keyboard (Girasoli and Hannafin 2008). Although such tools enable less vocal or shy students to participate in online discussions (Hewitt 2001), it poses a barrier to poor typists who find typing physically uncomfortable (Hammond 1999) and become frustrated using a keyboard (Girasoli and Hannafin 2008). A more significant barrier perhaps, as noted by Bowe (2002) is that text-based communication can be a challenge for students who have weak reading or writing skills; for example, students who are learning English as a foreign language. Inadequate English reading or writing proficiency could contribute to students' perceived information overload (Angelova and Riazantseva 1999; Eastmond 1995). This in turn could limit students' desire to contribute in the text online discussion. Such students find it very burdensome to read and respond to the online postings, and hence their participation tends to be minimal.

There is also some increase in cognitive load on students who have to concentrate on using a keyboard while trying to participate in a discussion (Girasoli and Hannafin 2008). For example, An and Frick (2006) found that this frustrated some students because it "takes too much time to type and complete a discussion" (p. 493), and hence students ceased to contribute further in the discussion. In addition, some participants find it difficult to express themselves or explain complex concepts using the text-based medium (Arend 2009; Hew and Hara 2007a). Moreover, participants may run the risk of being misunderstood easily in text discussion due to the lack of verbal cues (e.g., tonal) (Hew and Hara 2007b).

In order to overcome these drawbacks, some researchers and educators have begun to explore the use of audio-based asynchronous discussion. For example, Girasoli and Hannafin (2008) suggested that audio-based asynchronous discussion could allow students to speak more coherently and understandably, aided by the use of inflections and expressions that are missing in text-based discussion. The use of tonal cues such as inflections and expressions could potentially help the receiver understand a sender's

K. F. Hew and W. S. Cheung, *Student Participation in Online Discussions*,
DOI: 10.1007/978-1-4614-2370-6_9, © Springer Science+Business Media, New York 2012

message better and therefore reduce the risk of misunderstanding. Consequently, this may promote more student contribution in the online discussion.

The use of audio in online education is, of course, not new. However, although audio has been utilized for many years through radio, audiocassettes, compact disks, and recently podcasts, these technologies typically suffer from a lack of interactivity (Junor 1992). These technologies are essentially used to send or transmit information one way, usually from the instructor to the students. For example, in a review of podcast use, Hew (2009) found that the most common use of podcasting is limited to the instructor distributing voice recordings of lectures or supplementary materials such as assignment tips for students to review the subject matter at their own time and pace.

The use of asynchronous audio discussion, however, can provide a means for students to interact and discuss with one another. Similar to text-based discussion tool, audio-based asynchronous discussion is independent of time and geographical location. With tools currently available such as the Wimba Voice Board, students could simply speak a question or comment into a microphone and record it as an audio clip on a computer. No additional software or knowledge about audio editing tools is required (Yaneske and Oates 2010). Students also have the option of typing a text description to be appended to the audio clip. The clip would then be posted into a threaded organization of other audio clips (Girasoli and Hannafin 2008). Discussion posts can be exported in various audio formats such as MP3, WAV, and Speex audio. Figure 9.1 shows a sample Wimba discussion forum.

Besides the Wimba Voice Board, educators could also use VoiceThread (http://voicethread.com) for audio online discussions. VoiceThread allows participants to participate in discussions around images, documents, and videos (Brunvand and Byrd 2011). Participants could leave comments in five ways such as using voice through a microphone, text, audio file, or video through a webcam (http://voicethread.com/about/features/). Figure 9.2 shows a screenshot of VoiceThread, which was created by its developers (http://voicethread.com/?#q.b409.i848804) to give an introduction of how this tool could be used.

Researchers such as Akasha (2011), Brunvand and Byrd (2011), and Mandernach and Taylor (2011), among others have suggested that using asynchronous audio discussion can increase student engagement and motivation during the learning process. However, such claims are often made based on conjectures, rather than empirical findings. We found the number of empirical studies on asynchronous audio discussion is still relatively small. A recently conducted search (end of January 2012) using keywords such as 'asynchronous voice', 'asynchronous audio', 'voice board', or 'voice thread' on the Academic Search Premier, the education resource reference information centre (ERIC), and Google Scholar revealed only seven empirical-based papers that examined the use of asynchronous audio in the context of online discussion.

Almost all of these previous studies focused on disciplines such as language learning (e.g., learning Spanish or English as a second language), or communications studies (e.g., Cho and Carey 2001; Gleason and Suvorov 2011; Marriott and Hiscock 2002; McIntosh et al. 2003; Poza 2011; Yaneske and Oates 2010).

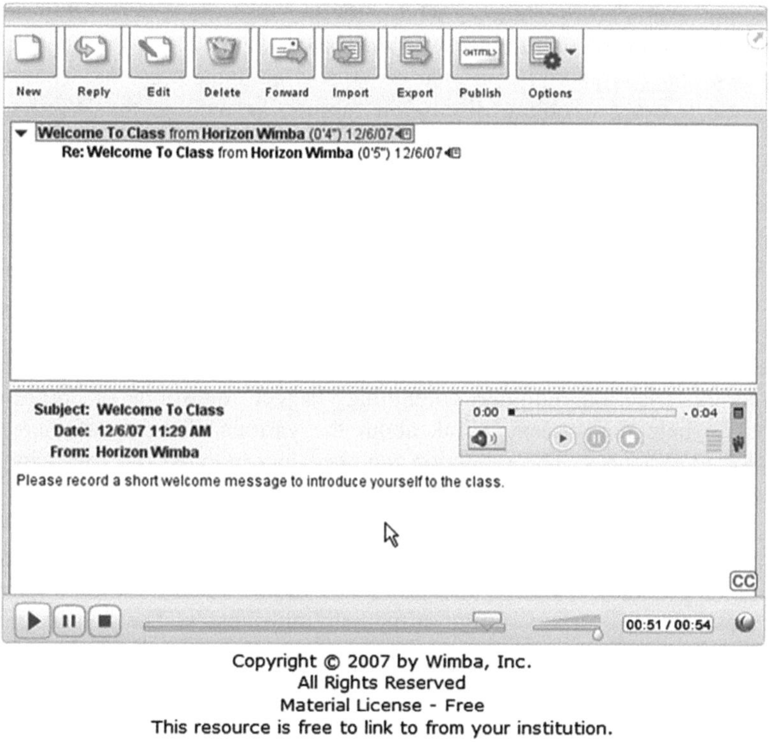

Fig. 9.1 Screen shot of a wimba voice board http://www.wimba.com/assets/videos/VoiceBoard/VoiceBoard.html)

Not surprisingly, the examination of asynchronous audio in these studies was mainly limited to how it could improve students' oral and listening skills, and whether it was easy and user friendly to use (e.g., Cho and Carey 2001; Gleason and Suvorov 2011; McIntosh et al. 2003). Only a few studies specifically examined the relative advantages or disadvantages of asynchronous audio versus text discussion (Marriott and Hiscock 2002; Yaneske and Oates 2010). Furthermore, none of the existing studies examined whether the use of asynchronous audio discussion could affect students' performance outcome such as their levels of knowledge construction. The dearth of data on asynchronous audio discussion therefore speaks to the need for more research in the area.

9.2 Descriptions of Studies 1 and 2

Recently, we conducted two studies to examine students' perceived benefits of using audio discussions, and their actual preferred mode of discussion (audio- or text-based) if given a choice. Moreover, we measured the levels of knowledge construction exhibited by students who participated in the text-based discussions and students who used the audio-based discussions.

The first study (study 1) consisted of 41 post-graduate students. The students utilized the text-based online discussion forums, as well as the Wimba Voice Board; both are available in Blackboard. Specifically, students in the first study used the text-based discussion forums first to discuss the following issue, "What are some strategies to engage students in web-based learning? Discuss the pros and cons of using these strategies", followed by the Voice Board forums to discuss the following question, "What are some implementation issues you may face when using technology in teaching and learning? What intervention or pre-emptive strategies could help? Discuss the strategies posted by your classmates".

At the end of the online discussions, qualitative data via student reflections were collected. A reflection template containing 'trigger' questions or 'probes' was provided to help the students think about the various elements of their online discussion experiences. The reflection template incorporated the following questions: (a) "What advantages do audio-based discussions have over text-based discussions?", and (b) "Given a choice, which one do you prefer to use? Why?"

The students' reflection data were then examined using the constant-comparative approach espoused by Lincoln and Guba (1985). The responses or comments were initially examined to group similar comments into themes. The fit between each student response and the theme was evaluated. Each theme was given a suitable label, and representative statements for each theme were selected and reported.

In the second study (study 2), we examined two classes. Class A consisted of 24 students while Class B comprised 18 students. Unlike the first study, all 42 students in the study II were undergraduates. Class A was randomly assigned to use the audio-based discussion first, while Class B used the text-based forum. The topic of discussion was "Do you think it is okay for people to buy or sell organs? Justify your viewpoints". After 2 weeks of discussion, the students switched the medium of discussion for another 2 weeks. Class A now used the text-based discussion while Class B used the audio-based forum. The topic of discussion was "How can teachers engage their students in online discussions?"

Similar to study 1, students in the Classes A and B were given a reflection template that contained the same trigger questions to help them think about the various elements of their online discussion experiences. The open-ended student reflection data were also examined using the constant-comparative approach (Lincoln and Guba 1985) to determine themes concerning the advantages of audio versus text discussions and students' preference for the medium of discussion. In addition, in study 2, we examined if students' mode of online discussion is related to their exhibition of and higher level knowledge constructions. Altogether the following research questions guided our investigations in study II: (a) What advantages do audio-based discussions have over text-based discussions? (b) Given a choice, would students prefer to participate in audio-based or text-based online discussions? Why? (c) What is the relationship, if any, between students' mode of online discussion (audio or text discussions) and their knowledge construction levels?

Table 9.1 Advantages of audio discussion (ranked)

Advantages of audio-based discussion	Rank
More expressive, able to detect emotions, understand someone better	1
Useful for participants with poor typing skills or students who prefer speaking to writing	2
More realistic, encourages participation	3
Spontaneity ensures originality of ideas	4
Better tool to assess how speech is delivered, or improve oral skills	5
Able to confirm identity of student	6

We examined the levels of student knowledge construction using each mode of discussion (audio or text) using Gunawardena et al. (1997) interaction analysis model. We referred the frequency of lower level knowledge constructions to the total number of phase I occurrences, while the frequency of higher level knowledge constructions to the sum of the number of phases II–V occurrences. An independent coder coded the participants' postings for knowledge construction. In order to determine the reliability of the analysis, another independent coder coded approximately 10 % (randomly selected) of the students' postings. The intercoder reliability of the coding for the audio and text postings were 90 % and 89 %, respectively.

9.3 Findings of Studies 1 and 2

9.3.1 Advantages of Asynchronous Audio Discussion

Comparing the two studies, our overall results showed that audio-based discussions have six advantages over text-based ones. Table 9.1 summarizes these six advantages. These advantages are ranked in terms of the frequency of each advantage being reported by the participants of both studies.

We can see that students most appreciated the opportunity to express themselves using the spoken word, and to hear the tone and voice used by the participants of audio discussion. This apparently helps participants to understand one another better because the spoken word can influence a learner's cognition by adding clarity and meaning due to the presence of intonation and the expression of emotions (Durbridge 1984). The following extracts from the reflection data illustrate this point:

> In my opinion, through voice-based discussions, students will be able to portray their feelings as well through the tones of their voice. This helps me listen to them to better understand what they are trying to say and their feelings about a certain issue. (Zoe, a participant in study 2)

This was corroborated by other students. For example, Pamela, a participant in study 1, remarked:

> Audio-based discussions allow the person's emotions to come through the discussion, so it is not just words. It is therefore less likely to misinterpret the words. Also, people have to listen to the entire audio to know the other person's full opinion or viewpoint, and so they are more likely to get everything, unlike text, which people tend to skim through.

The use of audio discussion is also particularly useful for participants with poor typing skills or who prefer talking to typing. This is consistent with Girasoli and Hannafin's (2008) observation. For example, Nora, a participant in study 2 explained, "It [audio discussion] can help participants who are not good with typing, and thus can save him a lot of time and effort in ensuring that he participates in the discussion". In addition, audio-based discussion is beneficial for students who prefer speaking to writing such as auditory learners, as explained by Participant Yeo, "It comes in handy for participants like me who are better in speaking than in writing. This will ensure that I'm able to raise my views clearly and avoid confusion".

In addition, audio discussion could foster a more realistic discussion environment that draws people into participation. Durbridge (1984) suggested that the spoken word can influence a person's motivation by conveying directly a sense of the person creating those words. Clark and Walsh (2004) highlighted that "listening is instinctual, [but] reading and writing are not" (p. 5). This suggests the ability of an individual's voice acting like a magnet that motivates people to join in the discussion who may otherwise not be interested in participating in the discourse at all. For example, Gee, a participant in study 1 explained:

> I feel that the degree of interest to participate in an audio-based discussion is higher compared to a text-based one because not only it is fun to hear how one sounds, but it also gives us a feeling that we are having a real conversation with the other party. This actually encourages us to listen to other people's opinions. The possibility for us to view another party's opinion in a similar fashion in a text-based discussion will be lower it as lacks this particular enticing factor.

Interestingly, we also found that the use of audio discussion could help promote originality of ideas. Results of our analysis suggested that this was mainly due to the impromptu nature of audio discussion. It appears that participants who use the audio discussion tend to think aloud whatever that comes to their mind with less reservation. In his study of oral versus text communication Ong (1982) argued that the former requires thinking which is more immediate compared to the latter. Compared to text discussion, participants have lesser time to plan beforehand what they want to say. As Elaine, a participant in study 2 explained:

> It [audio discussion] is more impromptu. Students tend to say what they feel and would provide a more realistic picture of views. With text based, students have the time to organize their thoughts and perhaps the end product might be one of high diplomacy yet of low insight.

This was echoed by Andrew, a participant in study 1:

> I feel that the participants' responses in audio-based discussions are more raw and real than rehearsed. Therefore, viewpoints seem more original and fresh, rather than appearing to be something that has been edited again and again [as in text-based discussions].

Table 9.2 Preference of participants

Type of discussion	Frequency	Percent (%)
Audio-based	27	36
Text-based	48	64

Note There were 8 students in total who either gave ambiguous answers or failed to answer at all. Hence, the inputs of these students were not considered

In addition, some participants reported that the use of audio-based discussions could help instructors assess how their students' speech is delivered. For example, Gina in study 1 explained, "For English Language teachers such as me, it can be a handy tool to assess my students for their speech, intonation, pronunciation, etc". Carol in study 1 also suggested that audio-based discussions could help students be cognizant of their own oral skill deficiencies: "Audio discussion also allows students to be more aware of which area of speech they will need to improve on". This was corroborated by Roland in study 2, "Audio-discussion provides participants the opportunity to develop their oratorical competence, something which cannot be done in a text-based environment".

Finally, one participant in study 1 highlighted that the instructor can find out if the person contributing in an audio-based discussion is indeed the actual person doing the voice post and not somebody else. This is unlike a text-based discussion because typing is more anonymous. Using an audio-based discussion can thus prevent cheating, especially if participation in the online discussion is awarded course marks or credits.

9.3.2 Students' Actual Preference

Interestingly, contrary to expectations and despite the reported advantages, students in both studies reported that they still preferred to use a text-based discussion if given a choice. A majority of the students (n = 48 out of 75, 64 %) indicated that they would use a text-based discussion (see Table 9.2).

Analyses of the participants' reflection data suggested four main reasons for the participants' preference for text-based discussion despite the reported advantages of audio discussion. Table 9.3 shows the four main reasons for this preference, ranked in terms of the frequency of each reason being reported by the participants of both studies 1 and 2.

The primary reason was that participants preferred to have more time to structure or organize their responses or comments before posting them online. It appears that the desire for structure or proper organization takes precedence over the desire for spontaneity of thoughts. The following two extracts from the participants' reflection data illustrate this point: "Typing allows me time to think, rethink, and vet through my response of how I want to put the matter across" (Lim, study 1), and "Given these two choices, I would use the text-based discussion,

Table 9.3 Reasons for choosing text discussion (ranked)

Reasons for choosing text discussion	Rank
Text-based discussion allows me more time to structure or organize my responses/answers	1
More convenient/ease of use with text-based discussion	2
Being self-conscious of how one sounds (e.g., horrible voice, unclear pronunciation, strong accent)	3
Typed words facilitate better learning/understanding	4

which allows more room for thinking and re-thinking" (Ho, study 2). This is probably due to the cultural context of our studies. All the participants in our study were of Asian ethnicity, with a majority of them being Chinese. Asian students tend to value social harmony and avoidance of conflict (Chiu 2009; Williams et al. 2001). This might have pushed them to want more time to edit their responses or comments for fear of offending someone. The impromptu nature of audio discussion might encourage them to say something which they might regret later. However, in text discussions they could edit and re-edit their comments many times, and this reduces the risk of accidentally posting any undesired comments.

Participants also found that text discussion is an easier or more convenient tool to use. This is mainly due to two reasons. First, the Wimba Voice Board tool does not allow participants to edit their recorded voice postings if they said something wrong. Participants have to delete the entire posts and record their voices again, as students Andrew and Yeo stated, respectively, "I find audio-based discussion more cumbersome to use because it does not allow students to edit the sound file. This means if I make a mistake, I need to start all over again. It will be good if the audio-based discussion platform allows participants to do editing", and "I'm unable to edit my voice if I say something wrong". Perhaps if such a function is made available in future releases of Wimba Voice, participants would find it more convenient to use.

Second, some participants found it inconvenient to listen to the whole voice recordings. They found it easier and faster to scan through printed words, as explained by Philip in study 2:

> I would still prefer a text-based discussion. Anytime I want to refer back to a thread posted by someone, I can just skim through the whole argument and extract the relevant stuff. However, for voice-based discussion, I have to listen to the whole recording.

We also found that participants preferred text discussions because they were self-conscious about how they sounded in audio discussions. For example, Loh in study 1 explained, "When recording my voice, I am conscious about my pronunciation and to make sure that I'm speaking in standard English, rather than broken English. This makes audio-based discussion quite tedious to me". This sentiment was echoed by Tang in study 2, "I prefer text based discussion as I feel awkward speaking into the microphone". Brick and Louie (1984) found that Asian students typically regard correctness as a highly desirable quality. Hence, they may fear appearing foolish by making mistakes such as unclear pronunciations if they

Table 9.4 Knowledge construction levels by asynchronous audio and text discussion

		Knowledge construction (KC)		
		Lower level	Higher level	Total
Text discussion	Observed	69	39	108
	Expected	76.1	31.9	108.0
	% within discussion mode	63.9 %	36.1 %	100.0%
	% within KC	44.5 %	60.0 %	49.1 %
	% of total	31.4 %	17.7 %	49.1 %
	Std. residual	−0.8	1.3	–
Audio discussion	Observed	86	26	112
	Expected	78.9	33.1	112.0
	% within discussion mode	76.8 %	23.2 %	100.0 %
	% within KC	55.5 %	40.0 %	50.9 %
	% of total	39.1 %	11.8 %	50.9 %
	Std. residual	0.8	−1.2	–
	Total knowledge construction	155	65	220

participate in the audio discussions, as these can have undesired consequences for them such as being laughed at by classmates.

Finally, some participants indicated that text discussions facilitated their learning better than audio discussions because they could not clearly hear some of the audio messages posted. For example, Lynn in study 2 remarked, "Sometimes I may not understand or hear clearly what my peers are talking because their voices are muffled". Other participants agreed, "I prefer text discussion. Sometimes I can't figure out what someone is talking because he or she has an accent or the noisy environment might not make what the person is saying audible" (Jim, study 2), and "Reading their postings give me a better analysis of the contents without the disturbance of external variables such as clarity of speech" (Nurul, study 1).

9.3.3 Possible Relation between Knowledge Construction Levels and the Mode of Online Discussion

Pearson Chi-square test of independence statistics suggested a significant relationship between the levels of knowledge construction and the mode of discussions (see Table 9.4): χ^2 (1, N = 220) = 4.393, $p < 0.05$, Cramer's V = 0.141. The data in Table 9.4 suggested that students produced more than expected higher knowledge construction levels during text online discussion. On the other hand, more lower level knowledge constructions than expected were produced during asynchronous audio discussion. In other words, the results suggested that audio discussions were more likely to yield phase I knowledge construction occurrences, while text discussions were more likely to foster phases II to V knowledge constructions.

Fig. 9.2 Screenshot of the voicethread interface

What are some possible reasons for this result? Recall that phase I refers to the sharing of information such as making statements of observation, or asking questions to clarify statements, while phases II to V refer to the exploration of dissonance of ideas, negotiation of opinions, testing, and application of ideas. Demonstrating phases II–V knowledge constructions typically require participants to challenge other people's opinions and ideas (Liu et al.2008). We posit that text online discussion may be more suitable for this because it allows participants a little more time to structure their responses. Additionally, some participants commented that text discussion provides them some measure of anonymity because they could post their messages using a pseudonym. However, in an audio discussion, it is difficult to mask one's own voice. This measure of anonymity could give participants greater confidence to challenge other people's ideas or opinions.

We wish to highlight that although higher level knowledge constructions are generally preferred in online discussions, researchers such as Hew and Cheung (2011) and schellens et al. (2005) posit that a necessary, if not sufficient, condition for higher knowledge construction levels to happen is to have a relatively large amount of lower level occurrences (i.e., phase I) in order to function as a starting point to ground the rest of the online discussion. Our results thus suggest that it may be best to combine the use of both audio and text discussions as the two platforms appear to promote phase I and phases II–V, respectively.

References

Akasha, O. (2011) Voicethread as a good tool to motivate ells and much more. In Koehler, M. and Mishra, P. (ed.) *Proceedings of Society for Information Technology and Teacher Education International Conference*, pp 3123–3127, Virginia: Association for the Advancement of Computing in Education.

An, Y.-J., & Frick, T. (2006). Student perceptions of asynchronous computer-mediated communication in face-to-face courses. *Journal of Computer-Mediated Communication, 11*(2), 485–499.

Angelova, M., & Riazantseva, A. (1999). If you don't tell me, how can I know?: A case study of four international students learning to write the U.S. way. *Written Communication, 16*(4), 491–525.

Arend, B. (2009). Encouraging critical thinking in online threaded discussions. *The Journal of Educators Online*, *6*(1). Retrieved on February 15, 2012 from http://www.thejeo.com/Archives/Volume6Number1/Arendpaper.pdf

Bowe, F. G. (2002). Deaf and hard of hearing Americans' instant messaging and e-mail use: A national survey. *American Annals of the Deaf, 147*(4), 6–10.

Brick, J., & Louie, G. (1984). *Language and culture—Vietnam: Background notes for teachers in the adult migrant education program.* Sydney: Adult Migrant Education Service.

Brunvand, S., & Byrd, S. (2011). Using voice thread to promote learning engagement and success for all students. *Teaching Exceptional Children, 43*(4), 28–37.

Chiu,Y-C. J. (2009). Facilitating Asian students' critical thinking in online discussions. *British Journal of Educational Technology, 40*(1), 42–57.

Cho, S. P., & Carey, S. (2001). Increasing Korean oral fluency using an electronic bulletin board and Wimba-based voiced chat. *The Korean Language in America, 6*, 115–128.

Clark, D., & Walsh, S. (2004). iPod-learning. [White paper]. Brighton, UK: Epic Group.

Durbridge, N. (1984). Media in course design, No. 9, audio cassettes. *The role of technology in distance education*. Kent, UK: Croom Helm.

Eastmond, D. V. (1995). *Alone but together: Adult distance study through computer conferencing*. Cresskill: Hampton.

Girasoli, A. J., & Hannafin, R. D. (2008). Using asynchronous AV communication tools to increase academic self-efficacy. *Computers and Education, 51*, 1676–1682.

Gleason, J., & Suvorov, R. (2011). Learner perceptions of asynchronous oral computer-mediated communication tasks using Wimba Voice for developing their L2 oral proficiency. In S. Huffman & V. Hegelheimer (Eds.), *The role of CALL in hybrid and online language courses*. Ames, IA: Iowa State University. Retrieved on January 18, 2012 from http://www.public.iastate.edu/~apling/TSLL/2010/pdfs/gleason_and_suvorov_2011.pdf

Gunawardena, C. N., Lowe, C. A., & Anderson, T. (1997). Analysis of a global online debate and the development of an interaction analysis model for examining social construction of knowledge in computer conferencing. *Journal Educational Computing Research, 17*(4), 397–431.

Hammond, M. (1999). Issues associated with participation in on line forums—the case of the communicative learner. *Education and Information Technologies, 4*(4), 353–367.

Hew, K. F. (2009). Use of audio podcast in k-12 and higher education: a review of research topics and methodologies. *Educational Technology Research and Development, 57*(3), 333–357.

Hew, K. F., & Cheung, W. S. (2011). Higher-level knowledge construction in asynchronous online discussions: An analysis of group size, duration of online discussion, and student facilitation techniques. *Instructional Science, 39*(3), 303–319.

Hew, K. F., & Hara, N. (2007a). Empirical study of motivators and barriers of teacher online knowledge sharing. *Educational Technology Research and Development, 55*(6), 573–595.

Hew, K. F., & Hara, N. (2007b). Knowledge sharing in online environments: A qualitative case study. *Journal of the American Society for Information Science and Technology, 59*(14), 2310–2324.

Hewitt, J. (2001). Beyond threaded discourse. *International Journal of Educational Telecommunications, 7*(3), 207–221.

Junor, L. (1992). Teaching by tape: Some benefits, problems, and solutions. *Distance Education, 13*(1), 93–107.

Lincoln, Y. S., & Guba, E. G. (1985). *Naturalistic inquiry*. Beverly Hills: Sage Publications.

Liu, X., Doore, B. & Li, L. (2008). Scaffolding knowledge co-construction in web-based discussions through message labeling. In K. McFerrin et al. (Eds.), *Proceedings of Society for Information Technology and Teacher Education International Conference 2008* (pp. 3041–3046). Chesapeake, VA: AACE.

Mandernach, B. J. and Taylor, S. S. (2011) Web 2.0 applications to foster student engagement. In Miller, R. L. et al. (ed.) *Promoting student engagement. Volume 1: Programs, Techniques and Opportunities* (pp. 220–229), Society for the teaching of psychology: Division 2, American Psychological Association.

Marriott, P. & Hiscock, J. (2002). Voice vs Text-based Discussion Forums: an implementation of Wimba Voice Boards. In Driscoll, M. & Reeves, T. (Eds.), *Proceedings of World Conference on E-Learning in Corporate, Government, Healthcare, and Higher Education 2002* (pp. 640–646). Chesapeake, VA: AACE.

McIntosh, S., Braul, B., & Chao, T. (2003). A case study in asynchronous voice conferencing for language instruction. *Educational Media International, 40*(1), 63–74.

Ong, W. J. (1982). *Orality and literacy: The technologizing of the word*. New York: Methuen & Co. Ltd.

Poza, M. S. C. (2011). The effects of asynchronous computer voicevoice conferencing on L2 learners' speaking anxiety. *IALLT Journal of Language Learning Technologies, 41*(1), 33–63.

Schellens, T., Keer, H. V., & Valcke, M. (2005). The impact of role assignment on knowledge construction in asynchronous discussion groups. *Small Group Research, 36*(6), 704–745.

Williams, S. W., Watkins, K., Daly, B., & Courtney, B. (2001). Facilitating cross-cultural online discussion groups: Implications for practice. *ETAL Distance Education, 22*(1), 151–168.

Yaneske, E., & Oates, B. (2010). Using voice boards: Pedagogical design, technological implementation, evaluation and reflections. *ALT-J Research in Learning Technology, 18*(3), 233–250.

Chapter 10
Future Research Directions

In this chapter, we propose several future research directions concerning the use of asynchronous online discussion in education contexts. These include the following possibilities: (a) examine the use of peer facilitation in different contexts, (b) investigate possible solutions to overcome the strategy dilemmas, and (c) examine the use of online discussion in mobile devices. We provide more information about these future directions in the following sections.

10.1 Implications for Future Research

10.1.1 Examine the Use of Peer Facilitation in Different Contexts

So far, the majority of studies on peer facilitation involved undergraduate or graduate students. We urge future research to examine peer facilitation strategies in asynchronous discussions used in different academic levels such as elementary and secondary schools, as well as corporate training contexts. In addition, the students who participated in our studies on peer facilitation should not be viewed as representing the whole population of students. It would be useful to replicate the studies in other cultures and countries to see if the reported findings apply. Future research should also conduct peer facilitation studies in other disciplines such as life sciences or engineering.

The 10 case studies described in this book (Chaps. 5–7) were situated within an ill-structured problem-solving (design task) activity whereby students owned and facilitated their individual discussion forums, and students had the freedom to choose to contribute in whichever discussion they wished without any posting quota being imposed. Future studies should investigate asynchronous online discussions involving different contextual elements from those delineated in our reported case studies. For example, future research could examine activities that

K. F. Hew and W. S. Cheung, *Student Participation in Online Discussions*,

DOI: 10.1007/978-1-4614-2370-6_10,

center on online class discussion of readings, or online debate of management philosophies. See Knapczyk and Hew (2007) for other possible online instructional activities.

Another possible direction for future research is to examine the use of asynchronous online discussion in fully online environments. A majority of the existing studies have focused primarily on blended-learning environments that combine face-to-face and online learning with reduced class seat time. In fully online environments, there is typically no face-to-face contact among students, or between students and instructors. Currently, blended-learning appears to be more appealing to students and faculty because it offers them some face-to-face contact time, as well as allowing faculty who are uncomfortable in a fully online environment to begin with a course that is mostly face-to-face before expanding the online session when their expertise in an online environment increases (Dzuiban et al. 2004).

However, some universities may be considering changing certain blended courses into fully online in order to reduce direct instructional costs further (e.g., reducing the number of computer labs, classrooms). Future research could investigate the peer facilitation techniques in completely online courses to see if there are variations in the facilitation techniques between blended and completely online courses.

Furthermore, due to the absence of face-to-face contact, the use of warm-up pre-online discussion activities (e.g., ice-breaking) may be very important to help students get to know one another (Hew et al. 2010). Future research could perhaps examine the effects of using warm-up prediscussion activities such as ice-breaking on student contribution in the online discussion. One example of an ice-breaking exercise involves students introducing themselves using eight nouns and then explaining why they choose each noun (Bonk 2004). Other students then respond to peers with whom they share common interests or experiences. An experimental research design could perhaps be adopted to assess the impact of such an exercise. Future studies could also explore other possible warm-up pre-discussion activities and examine their effects. This will help refine our understanding of how different warm-up activities might influence student contribution.

10.1.2 Investigate Possible Solutions to Overcome the Strategy Dilemmas

We urge scholars to continue to investigate possible solutions to overcome the guideline dilemmas. For example, with regard to the use of grades dilemma, we have earlier indicated that the mere giving of marks to increase contribution may not be a good strategy. One solution that has been proposed is to employ an evaluation rubric that spells out different marks for different specific categories of contributions. It is important to note that implementation of rubrics in actual practice may not be easy. We highlight two potential challenges that educators may face.

First, there are so many rubrics available for assessing student contributions to asynchronous online discussions, yielding a bewildering array of criteria as well as ratings (or definitions) (Jackson 2010). Penny and Murphy (2009), for example, analyzed 50 rubrics and identified 153 criteria and 831 ratings. Criteria refer to the specific elements or dimensions assessed by the rubric (Tierney and Simon 2004), while ratings "describe the way that qualitative differences in students' responses are to be judged" (Popham 1997, p. 1). In other words, ratings highlight the difference between different levels of performance (e.g., a performance assessed as fair or poor with one assessed as good or excellent (Penny and Murphy 2009). Faced with such a plethora of criteria, an instructor may find it difficult and time-consuming to choose a suitable rubric for his class to use.

Second, using a rubric to assess student contributions is subjective in nature. Unlike the award of marks based on quantitative measures such as the number of message posted or length of posts (which are easily measured by counting), rubrics contain qualitative descriptions of criteria across different performance levels (e.g., poor, fair, good, excellent) (Tierney and Simon 2004) which may not be easily understood or measured. Often, there are overlaps with the different criteria used. Furthermore, many readymade rubrics have basic consistency problems, meaning that the criteria change from one performance level to another level (Tierney and Simon 2004). Faced with such ambiguity, an instructor may be beset by problems of reliability when assessing their students' contributions. Therefore, the validity and reliability of using the rubrics evaluation approach requires further study.

Future research should also be conducted to examine the efficacy of the strategies described in Chap. 3. As previously mentioned, causal relationships between the implementation of the strategies and the successful reduction of student contribution problems in online discussions cannot be reasonably established at this juncture since many of the previous empirical studies were carried out using the descriptive research methodology, without employing control groups. Future research could perhaps adopt an experimental research design methodology to assess the cause-and-effect impact of using some of these the strategies.

10.1.3 Examine the Use of Online Discussion on Mobile Devices

Finally, no vision for the future of learning is complete until one discusses the possible convergence of digital and mobile technologies (Wagner 2006). Perhaps the greatest advantage of mobile devices is the convenience and portability that it affords to the students. For example, some researchers (e.g., Soloway et al. 2001) suggested that such devices have the potential to revolutionize learning, allowing students to undertake learning-related activities (e.g., online discussion) wherever they happen to be. Furthermore, because mobile devices are personal and portable, they may incite in learners a greater sense of personal ownership over learning

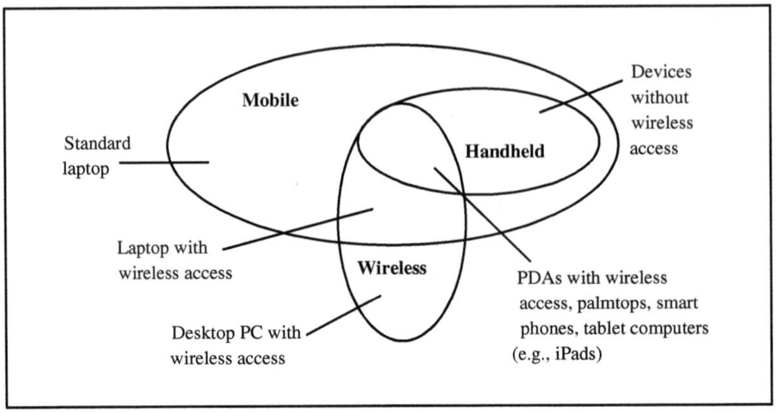

Fig. 10.1 Some examples of mobile devices (Cheung and Hew 2009)

tasks and the technologies used to support learning (Hennessy 2000). In addition, some course management system providers such as Blackboard™ have announced the launch of certain apps (e.g., Blackboard Mobile™ Learn) which allow students and faculty access to their materials on a variety of mobile devices including Android devices, Blackberry, iPhone, and iPad. According to Maurer (2011), Blackboard Mobile™ Learn allows students to create threaded discussion posts, among many other things.

Figure 10.1 provides a pictorial illustration of some mobile devices. However, in recent years, instructors and researchers are particularly interested in exploring the use of mobile devices such as smart phones, personal digital assistants (PDAs), and tablet computers, rather than laptops in education.

For example, Chang (2010) reported an empirical study that involved the use of mobile devices such as the Pocket PC in Taiwan. Specifically, the main purpose of the research was to determine students' acceptability of asynchronous online discussions on small-screen-sized mobile technologies. Altogether, two classes of information management students took part in the study. All students ($n = 32$) were given a Pocket PC each.

Recognizing that it was not easy for students to provide text-based input using Pocket PCs to an asynchronous online discussion forum, Chang (2010) experimented with the use of audio-based input. Students first logged into a discussion forum and read a question that had been posted earlier. Students then recorded an audio clip as a response to the question on their Pocket PCs. Students could post a message with their audio clips as an attachment to the asynchronous discussion forum. Listeners could then click on the clips to play the stream audio. This setup allowed students to listen and present their opinions in an audio-based mobile device asynchronous discussion environment.

At the conclusion of the study, a questionnaire based on the technology acceptance model (Davis 1989) was employed to measure the students' perceived usefulness and perceived ease-of-use of using an audio-based discussion forum on

Pocket PCs. Each student in the first class ($n = 16$) answered the questionnaire after using a text-based discussion forum and then answering the questionnaire again after using the audio-based forum. Each student in the second class ($n = 16$) did the reverse. They used the audio-based forum before the text-based one.

Interestingly, the results suggested that students' acceptance of audio-based input was not significantly higher than text-based input on a mobile device for an asynchronous online discussion. Moreover, there was no significant difference between a text-based and audio-based input in terms of perceived ease of use. However, students' perceived usefulness of audio-based discussion was higher than text-based on a mobile device. In other words, the audio-based input could be a better solution than handwritten input in an asynchronous online discussion environment on a mobile device in terms of usefulness. Further research studies should be conducted to examine the viability of conducting asynchronous discussions on mobile devices.

10.2 Epilogue

Many instructors and facilitators desire their students to contribute in asynchronous online discussions. However, this is easier said than done because limited student contribution appears to be a persistent and a widespread problem. In this book, we have attempted to surface the various factors that could lead to limited student contribution, the strategies to address them, as well as some of the strategy dilemmas.

Additionally, this book provides empirical studies on using students as peer facilitators. The concept of asynchronous online discussion is a rich and complex subject, and this book has revealed new perspectives on the concept especially with respect to possible ways or guidelines to encourage participant online contributions, sustain the discussions, and promote higher knowledge construction levels in peer-facilitated environments.

Taking a bird's eye view, these various guidelines may be categorized into three critical stages: Initialization, Engagement, and Closure. The Initialization stage refers to the activities that peer facilitators do before the discussion commences. Some of the typical activities include getting to know the participants (building relational capital), dividing discussion groups into about 10 members each, and choosing relevant and controversial open-ended discussion topic or question. Such activities help set the stage or orientate students to the online discussion.

In the Engagement stage, peer facilitators attempt to get other students interested in the discussion, keep them participating in it, as well as help them reach higher levels of knowledge construction. Typical activities in this stage might include displaying an open-minded habit of mind, contributing ideas and suggestions first instead of waiting for others to do (nurturing reciprocity), questioning, showing appreciation, encouraging people to contribute, and refraining from trying to resolve differences early in the discussion.

In the Closure stage, peer facilitators could summarize the main points discussed in the discussion and pose follow-up questions or set new discussion direction if necessary especially a continuation of the discussion is desired.

We also feel that this book has laid the foundation for a deeper understanding of the role of audio- or voice-based asynchronous online discussion. Given the importance of discussions in online- and blended-learning contexts, we hope that this book will be useful to other researchers and educators similarly engaged in efforts to enrich our collective understanding regarding student contribution in online discussions.

References

Bonk, C. J. (2004). The perfect e-storm: Emerging technologies, enormous learner demand, enhanced pedagogy, and erased budgets. Part 2: Storms 3 and 4. London: UK: The Observatory on Borderless Higher Education. Retrieved February 15, 2012 from http://php.indiana.edu/~cjbonk/part2.pdf

Chang, C.-K. (2010). Acceptability of an asynchronous learning forum on mobile devices. *Behavior and Information Technology, 29*(1), 23–22.

Cheung, W. S., & Hew, K. F. (2009). A Review of research methodologies used in exploring selected studies on mobile handheld devices in k-12 and higher education settings. *Australasian Journal of Educational Technology, 25*(2), 153–183.

Davis, F. D. (1989). Perceived usefulness, perceived ease of use, and user acceptance of information technology. *MIS Quarterly, 13*(3), 319–340.

Dziuban, C.D., Hartman, J.L., & Moskal, P.D. (2004). Blended LEARNING. Educause Center for Applied Research (ECAR) *Research Bulletin, 7*. Retrieved on February 16, 2012 from http://net.educause.edu/ir/library/pdf/ERB0407.pdf

Hennessy, S. (2000). Graphing investigations using portable (palmtop) technology. *Journal of Computer Assisted Learning, 16*, 243–258.

Hew, K. F., & Knapczyk, D. (2007). Analysis of ill-structured problem solving, mentoring functions, and perceptions of practicum teachers and mentors toward online mentoring in a field-based practicum. *Instructional Science, 35*(1), 1–40.

Hew, K. F., Cheung, W. S., & Ng, C. S. L. (2010). Student contribution in asynchronous online discussion: a review of the research and empirical exploration. *Instructional Science, 38*(6), 571–606.

Jackson, K. (2010). What value assessment rubrics in shaping students' engagement in asynchronous online discussions? In C.H. Steel, M.J. Keppel, P. Gerbic & S. Housego (eds.). *Curriculum, technology & transformation for an unknown future. Proceedings ascilite Sydney* 2010 (pp. 454–458). Retrieved on January 27, 2012 from http://ascilite.org.au/conferences/sydney10/procs/crisp-symposium.pdf

Maurer, M. (2011). Blackboard mobile apps reach nearly three million downloads. Retrieved on November 14, 2011 from http://www.blackboard.com/About-Bb/Media-Center/Press-Releases.aspx?releaseid=1618480

Penny, L., & Murphy, E. (2009). Rubrics for designing and evaluating online asynchronous discussions. *British Journal of Educational Technology, 40*(5), 804–820. doi:10.1111/j.1467-8535.2008.00895.x.

Popham, W. J. (1997). What's wrong—and what's right—with rubrics. *Educational Leadership, 55*, 72–75.

Soloway, E., Norris, C., Blumenfeld, P., Fishman, B. J., & Marx, R. (2001). Devices are ready-at-hand. *Communications of the ACM, 44*(6), 15–20.

Tierney, R. & Simon, M. (2004). What's still wrong with rubrics: focusing on the consistency of performance criteria across scale levels. *Practical Assessment Research & Evaluation, 9*(2). Retrieved on January 27, 2012 from http://pareonline.net/getvn.asp?v=9&n=2

Wagner, E. D. (2006). On designing interaction experiences for the next generation of blended learning. In C. J. Bonk & C. R. Graham (Eds.), *The handbook of blended learning: Global perspectives, local designs* (pp. 41–55). San Francisco: Pfeiffer Publishing.

Authors Biography

Khe Foon Hew is an assistant professor in the Learning Sciences and Technologies department at the National Institute of Education, Nanyang Technological University (NIE/NTU) in Singapore. Dr. Hew earned his PhD in Instructional Systems Technology from Indiana University in 2006. His research primarily focuses on online facilitation strategies, as well as student interaction, cognition, and knowledge sharing in online discussion environments. He has conducted many research studies on asynchronous online discussions since the year 2000. He serves on numerous editorial/review boards such as the British Journal of Educational Technology, Educational Technology Research & Development (ETR&D), and the Journal of Interactive Online Learning. He has won several awards including the 2006 ETR&D Young Scholar Award, and the 2011 IGI Global 4th Annual Excellence in Research Journal Award for having the Best Published Journal Article in the International Journal of Web-based Learning and Teaching Technologies. He has more than 85 publications including journal articles and book chapters to his credit.

Wing Sum Cheung is an associate professor in the Learning Sciences and Technologies department at the National Institute of Education, Nanyang Technological University (NIE/NTU) in Singapore. He is the program co-ordinator for MA in Instructional Design and Technology for NIE/NTU. Dr. Cheung earned his EdD degree from Northern Illinois University. His research primarily focuses on blended learning environment, asynchronous online facilitation strategies, and instructional design. He serves on a few editorial and review boards such as the Australiasia Journal of Educational Technology, British Journal of Educational Technology, New Horizon in Education, and International Journal of Web-Based Learning and Teaching. He has been researching in the area of "Asynchronous Online Discussion" for twelve years. He has published more than 100 publications including journal articles and book chapters.

K. F. Hew and W. S. Cheung, *Student Participation in Online Discussions*,
DOI: 10.1007/978-1-4614-2370-6, © Springer Science+Business Media, New York 2012

Appendix

Summary of Empirical Studies Reviewed

Author(s) and year	Method	Purpose of study	Sample	Data sources
Ahern et al. (1992)	Experiment	Investigate the effects of teacher discourse on the level and quality of student participation in an online discussion.	80 undergraduate students in an introductory educational theory and policy course	Online postings
An et al. (2009)	Quasi-experiment	Examine the effects of different instructor facilitation approaches on student participation	22 groups of undergraduate students (n=18, 18, 20 respectively)	Online postings, questionnaire
Arend (2009)	Case study	Explore how asynchronous discussions influence student critical thinking	29 students, 8 tutors	Online posts, interview
Bai (2009)	Case study	Facilitating student critical thinking using a critical thinking model as rubric	8 graduate students (fall 2007), 14 graduate students (spring 2008)	Online posts
Baran and Correia (2009)	Case study	Examine what peer facilitation strategies could increase participation and foster meaningful dialogue	16 graduate students in the USA	Online posts
Beaudin (1999)	Case study	Identify various techniques recommended and used by instructors to keep students on topic during online discussion.	135 online instructors	Questionnaire

(continued)

K. F. Hew and W. S. Cheung, *Student Participation in Online Discussions*,
DOI: 10.1007/978-1-4614-2370-6,

(continued)

Author(s) and year	Method	Purpose of study	Sample	Data sources
Beers et al. (2005) (computer script)	Quasi-experiment	Examine student online knowledge construction through the use of constraints/coercion	51 undergraduate students in the Netherlands	Online posts, questionnaire, interview
Bodzin and Park (2000)	Case study	Investigate asynchronous communication factors that influence the discourse of perservice science teachers	32 preservice secondary school science teachers	Questionnaire and interviews
Bradley et al. (2008)	Case study	Examine how different question types influence the quantity and quality of online discussions	114 undergraduates in the USA	Online posts
Brewer and Klein (2006)	Experiment	Investigate the effect of types of positive interdependence and affiliation motives in an asynchronous, collaborative learning environment	289 undergraduate business majors	Affiliation scale, online lectures, practice exercises, instructor notes, a posttest, attitude measure, and interaction checklist
Brown and Green (2009)	Case study	Examine the amount of time students spend participating in AOD	Graduate programs. Five discussion threads from each 21 course sections for a total of 105 individual threads.	Number of posts
Bullen (1998)	Case study	Investigate the degree in which students active participate in AOD and factors that affect student participation	13 undergraduate students.	Online postings, instructor interview, and student interviews.
Chanlin et al. (2009)	Quasi-experiment	Examine whether the use of labeled postings improve student online interactions	50 and 101 undergraduates in Taiwan, seven interviewees	Online posts, interview
Chang (2010)	Case study	Determine students' acceptability of using asynchronous online discussions on mobile devices	32 students majoring in information management	Questionnaire, interview
Chapman et al. (2008)	Case study	Examine student decision to respond to online discussion posts	21 graduates in the USA	Reflection survey

(continued)

(continued)

Author(s) and year	Method	Purpose of study	Sample	Data sources
Chen and Chiu (2008)	Ex post facto	Examine how earlier messages affect later messages	47 participants (undergraduates and graduates) in a Math discussion board in China	Online postings
Chen and Caropreso (2004)	Ex post facto	Explore the influence of personality on online discussion	70 undergraduates educational psychology majors	Personality test and attitude survey.
Chen et al. (2012)	Case study	Investigate the influence of students' perceived information overload on their participation and knowledge construction in online discussions	12 graduate students at a college of education	Questionnaire, online posts, interviews
Cheong and Cheung (2008)	Case study	Investigate lower secondary school students' critical thinking in an online discussion	35 lower secondary students in Singapore	Online posts, questionnaire
Cheung and Hew (2004)	Case study	Investigate the roles of asynchronous online discussion and reflection logs in supporting ill-structured problem solving	47 preservice teachers	Online postings, participant questionnaire, and participant focus group interview
Cheung and Hew (2006)	Case study	Examine how preservice teachers interacted with one another, as well as the types of thinking skills (critical and creative thinking) and levels of information processing (surface or in-depth) in an asynchronous online discussion	38 preservice teachers	Online postings, reflection logs, and focus groups
Cheung and Hew (2005)	Quantitative	Explore the factors affecting student satisfaction in using online discussion	47 preservice teachers	Survey
Cheung and Hew (2007)	Case study	Investigate the use of ground rules and guidelines in asynchronous online discussions	22 preservice teachers	Online postings
Cheung and Hew (2010)	Case study	Determine the situations in which students prefer instructor versus peer facilitation of online discussions	12 undergraduate students	Student reflections

(continued)

(continued)

Author(s) and year	Method	Purpose of study	Sample	Data sources
Choi et al. (2005)	Field experiment time-series control-group	Investigate the effects of providing online scaffold for generating adaptive questions to peers during online small group discussion	39 undergraduate students in turfgrass management course	Online postings, open-ended essay questions, online survey, and telephone interview
Cho and Jonassen (2002)	Experiment	Investigate the effects of message labels on participants' interaction during problem solving activities	60 undergraduate students in economics	Online posts, student essay
Cifuentes et al. (1997)	Case study	Understand why and how students participated in computer conferences	~100 preservice teachers	Online posts, and questionnaire
Darabi et al. (2011)	Experiment	Examine the contribution of four discussion strategies to learners' cognitive presence (knowledge construction)	73 undergraduates in the USA	Online posts
Dennen (2005)	Case study	Investigate how activity design and facilitation factors affect student AOD participation	Students and instructors of nine online classes taught by eight different instructors at seven universities	Instructor interview, student questionnaire, online postings, and course documents
Dysthe (2002) (peer)	Case study	To find out what kinds of interaction took place in an asynchronous Web-mediated discussion	10 post graduate diploma students in a philosophy class	Online posts
Ertmer et al. (2007)	Case study	Investigate the impact of peer feedback used as an instructional strategy to increase the quality of students' online postings	15 graduate students in an online technology integration course	Online postings, interviews, questionnaire
Fauske and Wade (2003–2004)	Case study	Examine the conditions that foster democracy, community, and critical thinking in computer—mediated discussions	29 preservice secondary school teachers	Online postings
Fung (2004)	Case study	Explore why some students are not participating actively in online discussion	83 graduate students in education from three courses	Questionnaire

(continued)

(continued)

Author(s) and year	Method	Purpose of study	Sample	Data sources
Gao (2011)	Case study	Examine if a concept map type of discussion forum would promote more postings and sustainability of discussions	16 graduate students in the USA	Online postings, questionnaire
Gerbic (2006)	Case study	Examine student perceptions about participating in online discussions	7 students (not reported level of students)	Interview
Gilbert and Dabbagh (2005)	Case study	Examine the impact of structuredness of AOD protocols and evaluation rubrics on meaningful discourse	87 graduate students from 4 classes of instructional technology foundations and learning theory	Online postings
Gleason and Suvorov (2011)	Case study	Examine students' perception of using asynchronous voice discussion for developing their second language oral proficiency	10 international students	Questionnaire, interview
Guzdial and Turns (2000)	Quasi-experiment	Explore how effective discussion can take place in computer-mediated discussion forums	studies. In Study 1, 17 CaMILE discussions and 18 newsgroups discussions in undergraduate classes were used. In Study 2, one CaMILE and one newsgroups discussion of an undergraduate computer science class were used	Online postings.
Hammond (1999)	Case study	Examine issues associated with participation in online discussion forums	Case 1: 22 staff participants; Case 2: 12 participants; Case 3: 24 graduate students	Online posts, interviews
Hew and Cheung (2003a)	Case study	Explore the degree of preservice teachers' participation in asynchronous online discussion	16 preservice teachers.	Online postings
Hew and Cheung (2003b)	Case study	Explore the quality of preservice teachers' quality of thinking in asynchronous online discussion	16 preservice teachers.	Online postings

(continued)

(continued)

Author(s) and year	Method	Purpose of study	Sample	Data sources
Hew and Cheung (2003c)	Case study	Investigate the use of asynchronous online discussion in designing hypermedia projects	48 preservice teachers	Interviews, student reflection logs, online postings, and questionnaire
Hew et al. (2005)	Case study	Analyze the use of six online pedagogical activities	36 teachers	Questionnaire
Hew and Cheung (2008)	Case study	Examine the facilitation techniques used by peer facilitators to sustain an online discussion	24 preservice teachers	Online posts, reflection data
Hew and Cheung (2009)	Case study	Investigate what habits of mind exhibited by facilitators might influence the degree of student contribution in asynchronous online discussion forums	20 discussion forums	Online posts, interview
Hew and Cheung (2010a)	Case study	Investigate the possible factors that might influence the amount of student contribution in online discussion forums	41 discussion forums	Online posts, reflection data, interview
Hew and Cheung (2010b)	Case study	Examine if certain facilitation techniques might foster higher knowledge construction levels	12 discussion forums	Online posts
Hew and Cheung (2010c)	Case study	Examine if group size of the online discussion is related to the frequency of higher knowledge construction levels	28 discussion forums	Online posts
Hew and Cheung (2011a)	Case study	Examine if group size is related to the occurrences of higher knowledge construction levels, if the duration of online discussion is associated with frequency of higher knowledge construction levels, and the differences between more successful versus less successful forums in terms of types of facilitation techniques	40 discussion forums	Online posts, reflection data, interview

(continued)

(continued)

Author(s) and year	Method	Purpose of study	Sample	Data sources
Hew et al. (2010a)	Case study	Examine students' critical thinking in online discussion	Ten graduate students	Online posts
Hewitt (2001)	Case study	Analyze the degree to which students and instructors write convergent notes, as well as explore student perceptions about their own synthesizing and summarizing practices	21 students (on average) from 3 online graduate courses	Questionnaire, online posts
Hewitt (2003)	Case study	Examine how online discussions evolve over time	92 students in five graduate distance education courses	Online posts
Hewitt (2005)	Case study	Investigate why threads die in asynchronous computer conferences	14 graduate students in education course	Online postings and questionnaire
Hewitt and Brett (2006)	Correlation	Investigate how class size might impact student note production and note reading in asynchronous online discussion environments	28 graduate classes of varying sizes	Online postings
Hewitt and Teplovs (1999)	Case study	Analyze the growth patterns in computer conferencing threads	Seven graduate distance education courses	Online postings
Hummel et al. (2005a)	Repeated measurements according to a simple interrupted time series with removal experimental design	Examine how to encourage learners in an asynchronous learning network to contribute knowledge	125 students.	Online postings.
Hummel et al. (2005b)	Case study	Examine the conditions for increasing participation	About 73 participants each week in the area of education modeling languages	Online postings
Jeong (2004)	Ex post facto	Examine the effects of response time and message content on the growth patterns of discussion threads	19 graduate students	Online postings
Jeong and Frazier (2008)	Experiment	Examine how the day in which messages are posted (early, midweek, weekend) affect the number of responses	27 graduate students in the USA	Online posts

(continued)

(continued)

Author(s) and year	Method	Purpose of study	Sample	Data sources
Jeong and Joung (2007)	Experiment	Examine the effects of message constraints and labels on argumentation and challenge in AODs	38 undergraduate students in an introductory educational technology course	Online postings
Jung et al. (2002)	Quasi-experiment	Investigate the effects of three types of interaction on learning, satisfaction, participation, and attitude	124 undergraduate students from three courses	Online postings, attitude scale, satisfaction scale, and student achievement scores
Kanuka et al. (2007)	Case study	Explore the influence of five instructional methods on the quality of student contributions to online discussions	19 undergraduate students	Online postings, coders' reflective journals
Kear (2001)	Ex post facto	Investigate students' use of threading in two different AOD systems	42 undergraduate students divided into seven groups	Online postings
Kear and Heap (2007)	Ex post facto	Identify the design features of AOD systems to alleviate information overload	About 85–87 answered the first feedback questions, 62–70 answered the second feedback questions, and 58–64 answered the third feedback questions. Only 11 answered the online survey	Multiple-choice feedback, and online survey
Khan (2005)	Case study	Uncover motivating factors influencing growth in participation	38 elementary and secondary education students	Focus groups, questionnaire, instructor interview, online postings
Khine, Yeap, and Tan (2003)	Case study	Investigate pre-service teachers' quantity of participation, types of message ideas, quality of interaction, and quality of thinking	42 teacher trainees	Online postings
Kienle and Ritterskamp (2007)	Case study	Investigate the impact of different moderation strategies on levels of student participation	12 students	Online postings, student focus group interviews, and audio files of moderator meetings

(continued)

(continued)

Author(s) and year	Method	Purpose of study	Sample	Data sources
Koh et al. (2010)	Case study	Examine the relationship between students' levels of knowledge construction in online discussion with respect to their participation in project-based learning	17 graduate students in the USA	Online posts
Kucuk et al. (2010)	Case study	Examine the relationships between students' learning styles and their level of contribution in online discussion	online postings (from n = 139 students), questionnaire (n = 43), interview (n = 5)	Online postings, questionnaire, interview
Lee et al. (2011)	Case study	Examine factors leading to the low number of postings	59 students (level-1 business students)	Online postings, questionnaire
Liu et al. (2008)	Case study	Investigate the use of a labeling prompt for knowledge construction	13 graduate students	Questionnaire, interview
Lu and Jeng (2006)	Case study	Investigate how preservice teachers constructed new knowledge, the extent of knowledge construction achieved, and how instructors facilitated the online discussion to affect knowledge construction.	2 sections of a distance education course. Section 1 had 11 students, and section 2 had 10 students	Course evaluation surveys and online postings
Marriott and Hiscock (2002)	Case study	Determine the viability of using voice-based online discussion forums as a means to stimulate discussion and student understanding of weekly readings	154 in year 2001, 124 in year 2002 communication course students	Online posts, questionnaire
Masters and Oberprieler (2004)	Case study	Explore student participation through curriculum articulation	311 Health Sciences students	Online postings and exam results
Mazzolini and Maddison (2003)	Ex post facto	Investigate the effects of instructor intervention on student participation in AOD forums	3 semesters — semester 2, 2000 (135 students), semester 1, 2001 (180 students), and semester 2, 2001 (200 students)	Online postings and survey

(continued)

(continued)

Author(s) and year	Method	Purpose of study	Sample	Data sources
Mazzolini and Maddison (2007) (instructor)	Case study	Examine how the role of the instructor (e.g., instructor participation rates, timing of instructor postings) relates to student participation and perception	postgraduate students, over 40,000 postings from a total of 375 discussion forums, questionnaire (about 500 responses)	Online postings, questionnaire
McIntosh et al. (2003)	Case study	Explore students' experience of using an audio online discussion tool—Wimba Voice Board	41 undergraduate international students taking English language instruction	Online posts, questionnaire
Murphy and Coleman (2004)	Case study	Explore students' experiences of challenges related to online asynchronous discussions.	20 graduate students.	Participant questionnaire, interview, and reflection
Murphy et al. (1996)	Case study	Analyze how students perceived and used online discussion forums facilitated by graduate students	Undergraduate students	Online posts.
Nandi et al. (2011)	Case study	Examine how active students are in online discussion forums and whether the degree of participation affects students' marks	299 and 346 undergraduate students	Online posts
Ng and Cheung (2007)	Case study	Explore the relative effectiveness of in—class online discussion and face to face, tutor led discussion in students' recall of concepts	43 preservice teachers	Questionnaire, students' recall of concepts
Ng et al. (2009)	Case study	Examine how peer facilitation techniques contribute to sustained discussion in asynchronous online discussions	16 graduate students	Online posts, questionnaire, interview
Ng et al. (2010)	Quasi-experiment	Explore the effect of online scaffolds in supporting ill-structured problem solving processes in online discussions	22 graduate students	Online posts
Nussbaum et al (2002)	Experiment	Investigate the use of note starters and elaborated cases to encourage counter-argumentation	48 undergraduates in educational psychology	Online postings and personality survey

(continued)

(continued)

Author(s) and year	Method	Purpose of study	Sample	Data sources
Oliver and Shaw (2003)	Case study	Explore factors that encouraged and inhibited student participation in asynchronous discussion	67 medical students	Questionnaire, content analysis, correlation
Painter et al. (2003)	Case study	Investigate the effects of different kinds of tutor intervention on student engagement in argumentation	Three tutorial groups of applied linguistics	Online postings and questionnaire
Palmer et al. (2008)	Case study	Examine the impact of using a formal assessment on student discussion	86 undergraduates	Online postings, student demographic data, student final unit mark
Poole (2000)	Case study	Examine the nature of student participation in a discussion-oriented online course	14 graduate students majoring in educational technology in the USA.	Online posts, questionnaire
Poscente and Fahy (2003)	Case study	Examine the characteristics of postings which succeed in triggering responses as compared with those which do not	Number of participants not reported. Participants came from 2 Master of Distance Education courses and 1 professional training course	Online postings
Poza (2011)	Case study	Investigate the influence of an audio online discussion environment on second language learners' speaking anxiety	35 undergraduate students majoring in Spanish, 4 were interviewed	Online posts, questionnaire, interview
Quek (2010)	Case study	Analyze high school students' participation and interaction in an asynchronous online project-based discussion	276 high-school students in Singapore	Online posts
Rollag (2010)	Case study	Describe effective and efficient ways to teach cases online through online discussion boards	number of students not reported	questionnaire, focus group, interview, online postings
Rourke and Anderson (2002)	Case study	Explore the effectiveness of peer teams to lead online discussions	17 graduate students	Online posts, interview, questionnaire

(continued)

(continued)

Author(s) and year	Method	Purpose of study	Sample	Data sources
Schellens and Valcke (2006)	Ex post facto	Examine to what extent does working in AODs foster knowledge construction	Nine discussion groups from 38 groups (n=300 undergraduate students of instructional sciences)	Interviews and online postings
Schellens et al. (2005)	Experiment	Investigate the impact of role assignment on knowledge construction in asynchronous discussion groups	286 undergraduate students in instructional sciences	Attitude survey, learning style inventory, and online postings. Online postings were randomly selected from eight groups
Schellens et al. (2009)	Experiment	Determine how requiring students to label their contributions by means of De Bono's (1991) thinking hats affects critical thinking	35 undergraduates in Instructional Strategies subdivided in groups of 6 team members	Online posts
Seo (2007)	Experiment	Examine the effects of peer facilitation on meaningful interactions in online discussions	174 undergraduates in introductory chemistry course in the USA	Online posts
Skinner (2009)	Case study	Explore why online discussion activities fail to inspire timely participation	25 undergraduates in the UK.	Interview
Strang (2011)	Quasi-experiment	Examine whether the use of Socratic questioning and conversation theory can result in high quality posts	103 graduate students	Online posts, final essay scores
Tagg (1994)	Case study	Examine the use of peer facilitation in an asynchronous conferencing environment	Graduate students	Online post
Tagg and Dickinson (1995)	Case study	Investigate the effects of tutor messaging in encouraging student participation	Six modules consisting of 2 groups of students for three terms	Online posting
Thomas (2002)	Case study	Examine student contributions in order to better understand the nature of online discussion	69 undergraduate students in Australia	Online posts, questionnaire

(continued)

(continued)

Author(s) and year	Method	Purpose of study	Sample	Data sources
Vonderwell (2003)	Case study	Explore the asynchronous communication perspectives and experiences of undergraduate students in an online course	22 preservice teachers	Interviews, e-mail transcripts, discussion transcripts
Wise et al. (2004)	Ex post facto	Examine if teacher social presence is related to student message length, perceived learning, etc.	20 graduate students	Questionnaire, online postings, final course product (a completed lesson plan)
Xie et al. (2006)	Ex post facto	Investigate the relationship among students' intrinsic motivation for participating in online discussion and other issues related to participating in an online discussion board	Study 1: 91 undergraduate students from six sections of an instructional technology course. Study 2: 32 undergraduate students from two sections of an instructional technology course	Intrinsic motivation inventory, motivation change questionnaire, attitude survey, computer/internet skill survey, online postings (study 1). Intrinsic motivation inventory, student motivation change interview, attitude survey, computer/ internet skill survey, online postings, and instructor interview (study 2)
Yaneske and Oates (2010)	Case study	Evaluate the use of a Wimba Voice Board to support asynchronous audio discussion	11 graduate students in a MA course entitled "Language Learning and Teaching with ICT".	Questionnaire, interviews
Yang (2008)	Quasi-experiment	Examine the effectiveness of Socratic dialogue on improving critical thinking in online discussions	145 undergraduates (experimental group), 133 undergraduates (control group)	Questionnaire, online posts
Yang et al. (2005)	Quasi-experiment	Investigate the effects of using Socratic questioning to enhance students' critical thinking skills in AOD forums	16 undergraduate veterinarian students	Critical thinking skills inventory and online postings
Yang et al. (2008)	Quasi-experiment	Examine the impact of structured Web-based bulletin board discussions on the improvement of students' critical thinking skills	23 undergraduate students in a veterinary course	Online postings and attitude survey

(continued)

(continued)

Author(s) and year	Method	Purpose of study	Sample	Data sources
Yeh and Buskirk (2005)	Quasi-experiment	Investigate methods that an instructor can use to facilitate students' participation	112 undergraduate students	Online postings
Yeh and Lahman (2007)	Case study	Examine pre-service teachers' perceptions of online discussion	Six undergraduates in educational technology	Interview
Yukselturk (2010)	Case study	Examine factors affecting student participation level in an online discussion forum	196 students (54 %) of students were undergraduates or graduates) 6 students were interviewed	Online postings, interview
Zhao and McDougall (2005)	Case study	Explore the influences of cultural factors on Chinese students' participation in asynchronous online learning	Six female education graduate students.	Interview data
Zhu (2006)	Case study	Examine the types of interaction and levels of cognitive engagement in four asynchronous online discussions	71 students from three colleges (undergraduates from the college of education and college of health professions, and graduates from the colleges of professional studies and college of education)	Online postings

Index

K. F. Hew and W. S. Cheung, *Student Participation in Online Discussions*,
DOI: 10.1007/978-1-4614-2370-6, © Springer Science+Business Media, New York 2012

MIX
Papier aus verantwortungsvollen Quellen
Paper from responsible sources
FSC® C105338
FSC
www.fsc.org

If you have any concerns about our products,
you can contact us on
ProductSafety@springernature.com

In case Publisher is established outside the EU,
the EU authorized representative is:
Springer Nature Customer Service Center GmbH
Europaplatz 3, 69115 Heidelberg, Germany

Printed by Libri Plureos GmbH
in Hamburg, Germany